The Constitution of the

Confederate States of America Explained

ഹൈ THE LOCHLAINN SEABROOK COLLECTION ഹൈ

Five-Star Books & Gifts From the Heart of the American South

SeaRavenPress.com

The Constitution

OF THE

Confederate States of America

Explained

A Clause-by-Clause Study of the South's Magna Carta

Lochlainn Seabrook

JEFFERSON DAVIS HISTORICAL GOLD MEDAL WINNER

SEA RAVEN PRESS, NASHVILLE, TENNESSEE, USA

THE CONSTITUTION OF THE
CONFEDERATE STATES OF AMERICA EXPLAINED

Published by
Sea Raven Press, Cassidy Ravensdale, President
The Literary Wing of the Pro-South Movement
PO Box 1484, Spring Hill, Tennessee 37174-1484 USA
SeaRavenPress.com • searavenpress@gmail.com

Sea Raven Press

Enlightening, educational, & entertaining books for the whole family!

1st Sea Raven Press paperback edition (978-0-9838185-8-8): May 2012
1st Sea Raven Press hardcover edition: January 2016

ISBN: 978-1-943737-15-4 (hardcover)
Library of Congress Catalog Number: 2012938264

The Constitution of the Confederate States of America Explained: A Clause-by-Clause Study of the
South's Magna Carta, by Lochlainn Seabrook. Includes an index and bibliographical references.

Front and back cover design and art, book design, layout, and interior art by Lochlainn Seabrook
All images, graphic design, graphic art, and illustrations copyright © Lochlainn Seabrook
Front cover illustration: "Confederate President Jefferson Davis and his Cabinet," Library of Congress

The views on the American "Civil War" documented in this book *are* those of the publisher.

The paper used in this book is acid-free and lignin-free. It has been certified by the Sustainable Forestry
Initiative and the Forest Stewardship Council and meets all ANSI standards for archival quality paper.

PRINTED & MANUFACTURED IN OCCUPIED TENNESSEE, FORMER CONFEDERATE STATES OF AMERICA

Dedication

To the Confederate Founding Fathers.
They lit the path for a world in darkness.

Epigraph

"When the people fear their government,
there is tyranny; when the government fears
the people, there is liberty."

THOMAS JEFFERSON

Contents

ARTICLE 2 - EXECUTIVE BRANCH

ARTICLE 3 - JUDICIAL BRANCH

ARTICLE 4 - CONFEDERATE STATES

ARTICLE 5 - CONSTITUTIONAL AMENDMENTS

ARTICLE 6 - GOVERNMENT & SUPREME LAW

ARTICLE 7 - RATIFICATION OF THE CONSTITUTION

The Montgomery Convention, February-March 1861, Howell Cobb presiding.

Notes to the Reader

THE TWO MAIN POLITICAL PARTIES IN 1860

☞ In any study of the "Civil War" it is vitally important to keep in mind that the two major political parties were then the opposite of what they are today. The Democrats of the mid 19th Century were Conservatives, akin to the Republican Party of today, while the Republicans of the mid 19th Century were Liberals, akin to the Democratic Party of today. Thus the Confederacy's Democratic president, Jefferson Davis, was a Conservative (with libertarian leanings); the Union's Republican president, Abraham Lincoln, was a Liberal (with socialistic leanings).

GRAMMAR

☞ To avoid overly cumbersome sentences, male nouns, pronouns, and adjectives (such as "he," "his," and "him") are used here to apply to both men and women.

TWO AMERICAN CONFEDERACIES

☞ America has had *two* different countries known as "the Confederate States of America": the original USA, formed as a confederacy under the Articles of Confederation in 1781, and the Southern CSA, formed as a confederacy under the Constitution of the CSA in 1861.[1] Although both are integrally connected (the latter was intentionally named and patterned after the first), this book concerns the latter.

TO LEARN MORE

☞ Neither slavery or Lincoln's War on the American people and the Constitution can ever be fully understood without a thorough knowledge of the South's perspective. As *The Constitution of the Confederate States of America Explained* is only meant to be a brief introductory guide to these topics, one cannot hope to learn the whole truth about them here. For those who are interested in a more in-depth study, please see my comprehensive histories listed on page 2; in particular, my title, *Everything You Were Taught About the Civil War is Wrong, Ask a Southerner!*

---

1. For more on this topic, see my book *Confederacy 101: Amazing Facts You Never Knew About America's Oldest Political Tradition.*

"Confederate Capitol," 1902 illustration. From far upper left, clockwise: Judah P. Benjamin, CS President Jefferson Davis, CS Vice President Alexander H. Stephens, George Davis, Stephen R. Mallory, John H. Reagan, Great Seal of the CSA, General Robert E. Lee, General Stonewall Jackson, George Trenholm, John C. Breckinridge. At the center is the Confederate Capitol. Bottom right: the USS Merrimac, originally a Union steam frigate, it was captured by the Confederacy, converted into an ironclad, and renamed the CSS Virginia. Bottom left: "Long Tom," a popular Civil War siege cannon.

Introduction

BIRTH OF THE SOUTHERN CONFEDERACY

Neither this book or the Constitution of the Confederate States would have ever been written except for one momentous and tragic event in American history: the election of the big government, South-loathing, Constitution-hating liberal, Abraham Lincoln, on November 6, 1860.

Knowing their constitutional freedoms were now at stake, the Southern states had little choice but to leave the US, which they began to do on December 20 with the secession of the first state, South Carolina.

With the inception of the new Southern Confederacy, a government was needed to oversee the people, and a constitution was needed to determine the powers and responsibilities of that government, and also to create, interpret, and enforce the country's laws, rules, and principles.

To this end, on February 4, 1861, fifty Southern delegates met at the state capitol in Montgomery, Alabama, to begin framing their infant government. This important gathering, known as the "Montgomery Convention," would give birth to a revolutionary new document: the Constitution of the Confederate States of America, the CSA.

After electing their convention president, Howell Cobb of Georgia, the Southern statesmen began debating the goals of the assembly. Having decided that secession from the Union was nonnegotiable and that conciliation with the North was unacceptable, they got down to the task of drafting a provisional charter that would contain the rules and regulations of the CSA.

Beginning February 5, a committee of twelve men, headed by Christopher G. Memminger of South Carolina, worked nonstop in secret session. The resulting document, which they built around the US Constitution, was presented to the convention on February 7, and on February 8, after a brief debate, it was adopted by unanimous vote. Thus was born the CS Constitution.

But the government which it was meant to form and regulate was not yet complete: it was time to vote in a provisional CS president and CS vice president.

On February 9, Jefferson Davis was selected as president, while Alexander H. Stephens was selected as vice president, both by unanimous decision. On February 11 Stephens was sworn in. On February 18, before a crowd of 10,000 people, Davis stood in front of the Montgomery Capitol, delivered his inaugural address, and took his oath of office.

For the rest of February, as the provisional CS Congress debated and passed laws, the twelve-man committee worked diligently to finalize and create a permanent CS Constitution. On February 28 the final draft was brought before the convention where it was debated over the next week and a half.

On March 11, 1861, with every detail finally agreed upon, the Confederate Founding Fathers unanimously adopted their work. From start to finish the CS Constitution had taken thirty-five days to complete. Officially, the Confederate States of America was now an authentic, constitutionally formed country of seven states: South Carolina, Georgia, Alabama, Florida, Mississippi, Louisiana, and Texas.[2]

In less than four weeks, a humiliated and fuming megalomaniacal Lincoln would trample upon his own Constitution and, tricking the Confederates into firing the first shot at the Battle of Fort Sumter, would illegally launch the so-called "Civil War."

COMPARING THE CS & US CONSTITUTIONS

Though the new Southern Confederacy based its Constitution on that of the US, and was in fact meant to be a continuation of the original Confederate States of America, or Confederacy (as the USA was officially called from 1781 to 1789),[3] there are some significant differences, beginning with the Preamble.

While the US Constitution begins: "We the people of the United States," the CS Constitution opens with its focus specifically on states' rights: "We the people of the Confederate States, each State acting in its sovereign and independent character . . ."

The CS Preamble also leaves out the US phrases: "form a more perfect Union," "provide for the common defence,"[4] and "promote the general welfare." And while the US Constitution never mentions the word God, here the CS Constitution not only calls Him by name, it invokes the "favor and guidance of Almighty God."

There are numerous other dissimilarities between the two documents as well, revealing the great social, cultural, and spiritual divide between South and North, a deep and wide rift that has existed between the two regions since

---

2. Virginia, Arkansas, Tennessee, North Carolina, and portions of Kentucky and Missouri, would also soon become members of the CSA, making a total of thirteen Confederate states.

3. See my book *Confederacy 101: Amazing Facts You Never Knew About America's Oldest Political Tradition.*

4. This particular phrase is included later, in the CS Constitution's Article 1, Section 8, Clause 8.

the settlement of Jamestown, Virginia, in 1607, and Plymouth, Massachusetts, in 1620.

For example:

- In the CS Constitution only CS citizens are allowed to vote in elections; in the US Constitution voter eligibility is left to the states.
- In the CS Constitution slaves are called "slaves," rather than "those bound to service," as in the US Constitution.
- In the CS Constitution CS representatives are allowed to represent 50,000 people, as opposed to US representatives who can only represent 30,000.
- CS state legislatures have the power to impeach federally appointed officials; in the US Constitution only the House of Representatives is imbued with this power.
- In the CS Constitution the CS president is given the power of the line-item veto; the US Constitution gives the US president no such power.
- The CS Constitution bans trade protectionism; the US Constitution does not.
- The CS Constitution prohibits what we now call corporate bailouts; by not mentioning them, the US Constitution allows them.
- When referring to dates the CS Constitution uses the phrase "year of our Lord"; the US Constitution leaves out the word Lord and merely states "the year."
- The CS Constitution permanently bans the foreign slave trade in March 1861; the US Constitution did not ban it until ratification of the Thirteenth Amendment in December 1865.[5]
- The CS Constitution is extremely concerned with the fiscal responsibility of Congress;[6] the US Constitution all but ignores it.
- The CS Constitution integrates the first ten amendments of the US Constitution directly into its clauses;[7] in the US Constitution they are grouped into a separate section called the "Bill of Rights."
- The CS Constitution prohibits "riders" from being attached to bills in Congress; the US Constitution disregards this.

---

5. Constitutional attempts had been made by Southerners, like President Thomas Jefferson, to rid the US of the slave trade by 1808. But Yankee slave ship owners and Northern businessmen ignored the ban, and the trade carried on in the Northern states right up and into the Civil War. For more on this topic, see my book *Everything You Were Taught About American Slavery is Wrong, Ask a Southerner!*

6. See in particular Article 1, Section 9, Clauses 9 and 10 of the CS Constitution.

7. See Article 1, Section 9, Clauses 12 through 19, and Article 6, Clauses 5 and 6, of the CS Constitution.

• The CS president serves one six-year term; the US president serves one four-year term and may be reelected (once) for a second four-year term.
• In the CS Constitution it is state legislatures who approve or disapprove proposed amendments to the Constitution; in the US Constitution this power is given to the US Congress.

Though many other differences could be itemized, this list illustrates the general dissimilarity in tone and objectives between the CSA and the USA.

While as a whole the CS Constitution is not radically different from the US Constitution, its unique Southernness and its conservative tone well suited both the independent minded Confederate people and the moderate Southern statesmen who led the country between March 11, 1861, and April 9, 1865.

FINAL WORDS
The obvious question is, would it serve us equally well today? In the opinion of traditional Southerners, absolutely.

Our modern US Constitution could certainly benefit from some of the CS Constitution's more innovative and forward thinking provisions, such as a one time six-year term for the president, a ban on trade protectionism, limitations on the fiscal powers of Congress, and a strict prohibition against corporate bailouts and government subsidies (then known as "internal improvements"). Most importantly, there is the CS Constitution's emphasis on small government and states' rights, conservative ideals that are more relevant now than at any time since the War for Southern Independence.

There is much more to the CS Constitution, of course. These ideas alone, however, make the South's Magna Carta worthy of in-depth study and reexamination, particularly in light of today's grossly oversized, overly powerful, overly complex, highly militarized central government—a type of government that clearly was never intended by either the US Founding Fathers or the CS Founding Fathers.

It is my hope that this instructive little book will help serve as a valuable educational guide, both to those interested in the history and powers of the CS and US governments, and those who are looking forward to the next great Southern secession. You will find me on the front lines.

Lochlainn Seabrook, SCV
Franklin, Williamson County, Tennessee, USA
May 2012, Civil War Sesquicentennial

The Constitution of the Confederate States of America Explained

A Clause-by-Clause Study
of the South's Magna Carta

TENNESSEE MADE

THE CONSTITUTION OF THE CONFEDERATE STATES OF AMERICA

MARCH 11, 1861

Preamble

We, the people of the Confederate States, each State acting in its sovereign and independent character, in order to form a permanent federal government, establish justice, insure domestic tranquillity, and secure the blessings of liberty to ourselves and our posterity invoking the favor and guidance of Almighty God do ordain and establish this Constitution for the Confederate States of America.

EXPLANATION: The Preamble sets out the goals of the people of the CSA. These goals are: to create a permanent central government, a judicial system insuring that the people are dealt with in an equitable manner, maintain peace, and obtain the favor of God so that the "blessings of liberty" will be handed down to future generations.

Article 1

Legislative Branch

ARTICLE 1, SECTION 1

All legislative powers herein delegated shall be vested in a Congress of the Confederate States, which shall consist of a Senate and House of Representatives.

EXPLANATION: Article 1 establishes the legislative branch (which creates the laws) of the CS government, its structure, and the rules it is to operate under. Based on the idea of the "separation of powers," Article 1 creates the CS Congress, which is to be comprised of the Upper House—the Senate, and the Lower House—the House of Representatives.

  While the CS Congress is invested with the power to make laws, the body itself serves under the auspices of the Southern people. As stated in Article 6, Clause 6, it is they who choose which laws will be enacted and enforced by the legislative and judicial branches, not Congress. This is accomplished through the act of voting, which allows the people to elect into office those congressmen who they believe will best represent them.

  The two branches of the CS Congress are to hold each other in check, avoiding the problems of corruption commonly associated with monarchical and socialistic styled governments.

  Finally, Article 1 sets forth the tenet that only Congress, *not* the executive branch (the president) or the judicial branch (the Supreme Court and the lower courts), has the power to make laws.

ARTICLE 1, SECTION 2, CLAUSE 1

The House of Representatives shall be composed of members chosen every second year by the people of the several States; and the electors in each State shall be citizens of the Confederate States, and have the qualifications requisite for electors of the most numerous branch of the State Legislature; but no person of foreign birth, not a citizen of the Confederate States, shall be allowed to vote for any officer, civil or political, State or Federal.

EXPLANATION: This clause lays out the makeup of that portion of the CS Congress known as the House of Representatives (the Lower House), declaring that it will be comprised of individuals elected by the people from their particular state every two years.

Also spelled out is the requisite that only legal citizens of the Confederate States of America are allowed to vote in elections.

ARTICLE 1, SECTION 2, CLAUSE 2

No person shall be a Representative who shall not have attained the age of twenty-five years, and be a citizen of the Confederate States, and who shall not when elected, be an inhabitant of that State in which he shall be chosen.

EXPLANATION: This clause gives the requirements for becoming a member of the CS House of Representatives: he must be at least twenty-five years old; he must be a citizen of the Confederate States; and he must live in the state in which he is elected by the people.

ARTICLE 1, SECTION 2, CLAUSE 3

Representatives and direct taxes shall be apportioned among the several States, which may be included within this Confederacy, according to their respective numbers, which shall be determined by adding to the whole number of free persons, including those bound to service for a term of years, and excluding Indians not taxed, three-fifths of all slaves. The actual enumeration shall be made within three years after the first meeting of the Congress of the Confederate States, and within every subsequent term of ten years, in such manner as they shall by law direct. The number of Representatives shall not exceed one for every fifty thousand, but each State shall have at least one Representative; and until such enumeration shall be made, the State of South Carolina shall be entitled to choose six; the State of Georgia ten; the State of Alabama nine; the State of Florida two; the State of Mississippi seven; the State of Louisiana six; and the State of Texas six.

EXPLANATION: This lengthy clause focuses on how the individual states are to be represented in the CS Congress. This is to be done according to a state's free population, which will be determined by a national census conducted every ten years. At the time, a state representative could represent up to 50,000 people. Thus a highly populous state could have a number of representatives. But even states with less than 50,000 people are entitled to have at least one member in the Lower House. The purpose of the Confederate Founding Fathers here is to create the smallest congressional body possible.

"Those bound to service" refers to servants ("slaves" to non-Southerners), each one being considered "three fifths" of a person in order to prevent servant-heavy states from being over represented in Congress. Non-taxed Native-Americans were excluded from the decennial census.

Based on the current population of the original seven Confederate states at the time, each is accorded a specific number of representatives: South Carolina six; Georgia ten; Alabama nine; Florida two; Mississippi seven; Louisiana six; and Texas six.

Finally, this clause stipulates that direct taxes (as opposed to indirect taxes—such as congressional duties, excises, and imposts that are placed on businesses and business transactions) are to be paid by individuals directly to the government, and that direct taxation are to be apportioned throughout the Confederate states in the same way that state representatives are: by population.

ARTICLE 1, SECTION 2, CLAUSE 4

> When vacancies happen in the representation from any
> State the executive authority thereof shall issue writs of
> election to fill such vacancies.

EXPLANATION: This clause provides for unexpected deaths and resignations among state representatives, stipulating that the "executive authority," that is, the governor of the state to which the absent representative belongs, must call a special election in order to choose someone to fill the vacancy.

There is an exception to this rule, however: if a normal election is approaching, the ordinary process of public voting is to be used.

ARTICLE 1, SECTION 2, CLAUSE 5

The House of Representatives shall choose their Speaker and other officers; and shall have the sole power of impeachment; except that any judicial or other Federal officer, resident and acting solely within the limits of any State, may be impeached by a vote of two-thirds of both branches of the Legislature thereof.

EXPLANATION: This clause gives the CS House of Representatives the power to select its own leader, known as the "speaker," along with the other lower officers, such as the clerk of the house, chaplain, and sergeant at arms.

Additionally, this clause gives state legislatures the power to criminally charge any federally appointed state court official, such as a judge, with a two-thirds vote. According to Article 2, Section 4 of the CS Constitution, such transgressions include "treason, bribery, or other high crimes or misdemeanors." According to Article 1, Section 3, Clause 6, after impeachment, the individual is to be prosecuted by the House of Representatives before the Senate, the latter serving as both judge and jury.

As the speaker of the House is third in the line of presidential succession (in other words, he would take over as president if both the Confederate president and the Confederate vice president died), this clause assures the country's citizens of a well qualified speaker, along with honorable and reliable government officials.

ARTICLE 1, SECTION 3, CLAUSE 1

The Senate of the Confederate States shall be composed of two Senators from each State, chosen for six years by the Legislature thereof, at the regular session next immediately preceding the commencement of the term of service; and each Senator shall have one vote.

EXPLANATION: This clause sets up the composition of the CS Senate by spelling out how many senators each state can have (two), how long they will serve (six years), how they are to be chosen (by the legislature), when they will be appointed (during the last session just before their term runs out), and how many votes each senator is allowed to have (one).

The intention of this clause is to help protect small, low population states from being politically overwhelmed in the CS Congress by large, densely populated states.

ARTICLE 1, SECTION 3, CLAUSE 2

Immediately after they shall be assembled, in consequence of the first election, they shall be divided as equally as may be into three classes. The seats of the Senators of the first class shall be vacated at the expiration of the second year; of the second class at the expiration of the fourth year; and of the third class at the expiration of the sixth year; so that one-third may be chosen every second year; and if vacancies happen by resignation, or otherwise, during the recess of the Legislature of any State, the Executive thereof may make temporary appointments until the next meeting of the Legislature, which shall then fill such vacancies.

EXPLANATION: This clause states that the Senate is to be divided into three sections:

1) Newly elected senators with six year terms ahead of them.

2) Senators elected two years previously with four year terms left.

3) Senators elected four years previously with two year terms left.

This allowed the public to reexamine the Senate, as well as vote in one-third of its membership, every two years. The aim is to keep the Senate filled with knowledgeable and experienced senators at all times.

This clause also stipulates that if a senator resigns during his term, the governor may make a temporary appointment. In such a case, however, the governor's selection would last only until the next legislative meeting, at which time the vacancy would be officially filled by that body.

ARTICLE 1, SECTION 3, CLAUSE 3

No person shall be a Senator who shall not have attained the age of thirty years, and be a citizen of the Confederate States; and who shall not, then elected, be an inhabitant of the State for which he shall be chosen.

EXPLANATION: This clause lays out the requirements for a Confederate state senator:

1) He must be at least thirty years old.

2) He must be a citizen of the Confederate States of America.

3) He must live in the state he intends to represent.

These requirements help assure the Confederate people of getting well qualified senators.

ARTICLE 1, SECTION 3, CLAUSE 4

The Vice President of the Confederate States shall be president of the Senate, but shall have no vote unless they be equally divided.

EXPLANATION: This clause gives the Confederate vice president his only real responsibility: he is to serve as president of the Senate. Also, in case of a tie in the Senate, the vice president may cast a single vote to break it.

By making the vice president the president of the Senate, the CS Constitution helps insure that the second most powerful individual in the CS government is up to date on current issues and affairs in the event that he needs to take over as president.

ARTICLE 1, SECTION 3, CLAUSE 5

The Senate shall choose their other officers; and also a president pro tempore in the absence of the Vice President, or when he shall exercise the office of President of the Confederate states.

EXPLANATION: This clause authorizes the Senate to select its own subordinate officers, as well as a temporary president in case the CS vice president is no longer available. In English the Latin term *pro tempore* means "for the time being"; that is, "temporarily."

ARTICLE 1, SECTION 3, CLAUSE 6

The Senate shall have the sole power to try all impeachments. When sitting for that purpose, they shall be on oath or affirmation. When the President of the Confederate States is tried, the Chief Justice shall preside; and no person shall be convicted without the concurrence of two-thirds of the members present.

EXPLANATION: This clause stipulates that, after the House of Representatives impeaches a government official, it is the Senate's responsibility to try the accused. This is to be done under oath.

In a case where the CS president is charged with a crime, the chief justice is ordered to preside over the judicial proceedings.

Lastly, no one can be convicted without two-thirds of the Senate agreeing on the final judgement.

ARTICLE 1, SECTION 3, CLAUSE 7

Judgment in cases of impeachment shall not extend further than to removal from office, and disqualification to hold any office of honor, trust, or profit under the Confederate States; but the party convicted shall, nevertheless, be liable and subject to indictment, trial, judgment, and punishment according to law.

EXPLANATION: This clause states that there are limitations on the type of punishment the CS Senate can impose on an impeached government official: he can be removed from office, and he can be barred from holding any governmental position in the future. Nothing more.

After the Senate has finalized its procedure against the defendant, he is subject to the regular laws of the land, including being formally charged, accused, tried, judged, and punished.

ARTICLE 1, SECTION 4, CLAUSE 1

The times, places, and manner of holding elections for Senators and Representatives shall be prescribed in each State by the Legislature thereof, subject to the provisions of this Constitution; but the Congress may, at any time, by law, make or alter such regulations, except as to the times and places of choosing Senators.

EXPLANATION: This clause stipulates that regulations regarding state elections are to be left up to the individual states, and that these rules are to be made according to the CS Constitution.

The CS Congress may, "at any time," create or alter the election rules made by the states. However, it does not have the power to change the times or places a state chooses to select its senators (as this is already set out in Article 1, Section 3, Clause 1).

ARTICLE 1, SECTION 4, CLAUSE 2

The Congress shall assemble at least once in every year; and such meeting shall be on the first Monday in December, unless they shall, by law, appoint a different day.

EXPLANATION: This clause specifies that the CS Congress must meet at least once a year. Additionally, the body must gather on the first Monday of December—unless a different day is lawfully selected.

The purpose of this clause is threefold:

1) To make members of the CS Congress work hard and earn their salaries.

2) To motivate congressmen to stay on top of governmental issues.

3) To prevent the executive branch (that is, the CS president) from prohibiting congressional assemblies or refusing to call Congress into session.

ARTICLE 1, SECTION 5, CLAUSE 1

Each House shall be the judge of the elections, returns, and qualifications of its own members, and a majority of each shall constitute a quorum to do business; but a smaller number may adjourn from day to day, and may be authorized to compel the attendance of absent members, in such manner and under such penalties as each House may provide.

EXPLANATION: This clause stipulates that both the Senate and the House of Representatives will be in charge of evaluating the elections, reports, and eligibility of their own members, and that a majority of each body will be considered a "quorum," whose main function is to handle business. A minority from each body, however, may close down their respective House, or force absent members to attend sessions.

ARTICLE 1, SECTION 5, CLAUSE 2

Each House may determine the rules of its proceedings, punish its members for disorderly behavior, and, with the concurrence of two-thirds of the whole number, expel a member.

EXPLANATION: This clause specifies that the CS Senate and the CS House of Representatives are free to create their own rules, penalize their members as they see fit, and remove from office who they like—as long as two-thirds of each body agrees.

ARTICLE 1, SECTION 5, CLAUSE 3

Each House shall keep a journal of its proceedings, and from time to time publish the same, excepting such parts as may in their judgment require secrecy; and the yeas and nays of the members of either House, on any question, shall, at the desire of one-fifth of those present, be entered on the journal.

EXPLANATION: According to this clause, the CS Senate and the CS House of Representatives must keep a record of their meetings, chronicles that must be made available for public review. The Houses have the authority, however, to keep parts of their proceedings private if deemed necessary.

While the actual words of CS congressmen do not need to be recorded in the House journals, the manner in which they vote can be, particularly if one-fifth of those present request it.

ARTICLE 1, SECTION 5, CLAUSE 4

Neither House, during the session of Congress, shall, without the consent of the other, adjourn for more than three days, nor to any other place than that in which the two Houses shall be sitting.

EXPLANATION: This clause states that neither the CS Senate or the CS House of Representatives can take a break for more than three days without the authorization of the other body.

Additionally, neither the Senate or the House of Representatives can meet any place other than the CS Capitol Building without the authorization of the other body.

ARTICLE 1, SECTION 6, CLAUSE 1

The Senators and Representatives shall receive a compensation for their services, to be ascertained by law, and paid out of the Treasury of the Confederate States. They shall, in all cases, except treason, felony, and breach of the peace, be privileged from arrest during their attendance at the session of their respective Houses, and in going to and returning from the same; and for any speech or debate in either House, they shall not be questioned in any other place.

EXPLANATION: This clause begins by stipulating that members of the CS Senate and the CS House of Representatives will be paid for their time, the amount which is to be determined by they themselves. They will be paid by the CS Treasury.

In order to allow true freedom of expression in the CS Congress, this clause also gives Confederate congressmen immunity from arrest for anything they might say while on the floor. However, they can still be arrested for committing treason or a felony, or for disturbing the peace.

ARTICLE 1, SECTION 6, CLAUSE 2

No Senator or Representative shall, during the time for which he was elected, be appointed to any civil office under the authority of the Confederate States, which shall have been created, or the emoluments whereof shall have been increased during such time; and no person holding any office under the Confederate States shall be a member of either House during his continuance in office. But Congress may, by law, grant to the principal officer in each of the Executive Departments a seat upon the floor of either House, with the privilege of discussing any measures appertaining to his department.

EXPLANATION: This clause orders that a CS senator or a representative cannot serve in both Congress and in the executive branch simultaneously, or resign in order to take a new governmental job he has helped create or which has increased in salary while he was in office. He must wait until his term has expired.

Also, the "principal officer in each of the Executive Departments," that is, the Confederate cabinet secretaries, may attend, or can be called to attend, sessions in either the Senate or the House of Representatives, to discuss their own opinions or answer questions.

ARTICLE 1, SECTION 7, CLAUSE 1

All bills for raising revenue shall originate in the House of Representatives; but the Senate may propose or concur with amendments, as on other bills.

EXPLANATION: This clause sets up the process of congressional lawmaking. A bill can come from either House, but the creation of bills that would burden the Confederate populace with taxation specifically must come from the House of Representatives. For it is this branch that is most closely tied to the Southern people, both politically and personally.

ARTICLE 1, SECTION 7, CLAUSE 2

Every bill which shall have passed both Houses, shall, before it becomes a law, be presented to the President of the Confederate States; if he approve, he shall sign it; but if not, he shall return it, with his objections, to that House in which it shall have originated, who shall enter the objections at large on their journal, and proceed to reconsider it. If, after such reconsideration, two-thirds of that House shall agree to pass the bill, it shall be sent, together with the objections, to the other House, by which it shall likewise be reconsidered, and if approved by two-thirds of that House, it shall become a law. But in all such cases, the votes of both Houses shall be determined by yeas and nays, and the names of the persons voting for and against the bill shall be entered on the journal of each House respectively. If any bill shall not be returned by the President within ten days (Sundays excepted) after it shall have been presented to him, the same shall be a law, in like manner as if he had signed it, unless the Congress, by their adjournment, prevent its return; in which case it shall not be a law. The President may approve any appropriation and disapprove any other appropriation in the same bill. In such case he shall, in signing the bill, designate the appropriations disapproved; and shall return a copy of such appropriations, with his objections, to the House in which the bill shall have originated; and the same proceedings shall then be had as in case of other bills disapproved by the President.

EXPLANATION: Known as the "Presentment Clause," this clause stipulates that after a bill has passed through both the Senate and the House of Representatives, it must be submitted to the CS president for his approval. If approved, he signs the bill and it becomes law. If not approved, he vetoes it, sending it back to the original House with his objections. That House must then record the president's objections in their daily report and then reexamine the bill.

If two-thirds of that House now approve the bill, they must send it to the other House for examination. If two-thirds of the second House approve it, the president's veto is overridden and the bill becomes law.

Voting is to be done by "yeas" and "nays," and all of the names of the voting congressmen are to be written down in the report of each individual House.

After a bill has been presented to the Confederate president, he has only ten days (Sundays are not counted) to look it over and return it to the House in which it originated. If he fails to return the bill within the proscribed ten days, it automatically becomes law—unless the CS Congress is in adjournment (which would, of course, prevent it from being delivered).

Finally, this clause gives the CS president the power to approve any portion of a bill into law while disapproving any other portion. Though not known by this name at the time, today this power is called a line-item veto—a power not given to the US president by the US Constitution.

ARTICLE 1, SECTION 7, CLAUSE 3

Every order, resolution, or vote, to which the concurrence of both Houses may be necessary (except on a question of adjournment) shall be presented to the President of the Confederate States; and before the same shall take effect, shall be approved by him; or, being disapproved by him, shall be repassed by two-thirds of both Houses, according to the rules and limitations prescribed in case of a bill.

EXPLANATION: This clause, Clause 3, is something of a restatement and further clarification of Clause 2. It stipulates that *all* orders, resolutions, and votes that need a two-thirds vote from both Houses (excluding "a question of adjournment") must be presented to the CS president. Otherwise, they cannot become law.

In case the president disapproves a bill, both Houses can pass it anyway, as long as they follow the rules for amendment making as laid down in the CS Constitution.[8]

---

8. See Article 5.

ARTICLE 1, SECTION 8, CLAUSE 1

The Congress shall have power to lay and collect taxes, duties, imposts, and excises for revenue, necessary to pay the debts, provide for the common defense, and carry on the Government of the Confederate States; but no bounties shall be granted from the Treasury; nor shall any duties or taxes on importations from foreign nations be laid to promote or foster any branch of industry; and all duties, imposts, and excises shall be uniform throughout the Confederate States.

EXPLANATION: This entire section, Section 8, is devoted to listing Congress' powers, known as the "enumerated powers" of Congress.

Beginning with Clause 1, the CS Constitution gives Congress the power to impose and collect indirect taxes in order to pay the nation's debts, provide for a military, and help pay the cost of running the Confederate government.

In response to decades of abuse by the North, which often used protectionist laws to prevent the South from purchasing inexpensive foreign products, this clause bans trade protectionism and also bounties. This means that taxes cannot be placed on imported goods in order to promote or protect Confederate businesses. In addition, government subsidies ("bounties")—that is, financial assistance—cannot be given out by the CS Treasury to private industries. This is intended to prevent the government from using taxpayers' money to prop up unprofitable businesses.

Lastly, any and all tariffs, taxes, and excises issued by Congress must be the same throughout all of the Confederate states. In other words, Congress cannot make a tax on guns higher or lower in a particular state. It must be the same amount in all of the Confederate states.

ARTICLE 1, SECTION 8, CLAUSE 2

The Congress shall have power to borrow money on the credit of the Confederate States.

EXPLANATION: This clause allows the CS Congress to accept loans from the CS government (that is, from the taxpayers), which it pledges to pay back in deferred payments. This money is used to sustain the government, which in turn provides numerous services to the Confederate people.

ARTICLE 1, SECTION 8, CLAUSE 3

The Congress shall have power to regulate commerce with foreign nations, and among the several States, and with the Indian tribes; but neither this, nor any other clause contained in the Constitution, shall ever be construed to delegate the power to Congress to appropriate money for any internal improvement intended to facilitate commerce; except for the purpose of furnishing lights, beacons, and buoys, and other aids to navigation upon the coasts, and the improvement of harbors and the removing of obstructions in river navigation; in all which cases such duties shall be laid on the navigation facilitated thereby as may be necessary to pay the costs and expenses thereof.

EXPLANATION: This clause allows the CS Congress to oversee trade between foreign countries and with both the Confederate states and with Native-Americans. Control of international commerce also gives Congress the power to issue regulations regarding imports and exports, as well as immigration and emigration.

"Internal improvements," or what we now call corporate bailouts or government subsidies, however, are prohibited. This means that Congress cannot use money to assist private industry, in essence, blocking the CS government from funding big business. Government money (that is, taxpayers' money) is to be used to serve the people only.

While bailouts for private businesses are strictly banned, this clause makes one exception to this rule. It allows Congress to loan money to companies and businesses involved in river navigation and sea trade, each important aspects of the Southern economy—much of which has always been based around Dixie's many seaports and her 3,600 miles of coastline.

ARTICLE 1, SECTION 8, CLAUSE 4

The Congress shall have power to establish uniform laws of naturalization, and uniform laws on the subject of bankruptcies, throughout the Confederate States; but no law of Congress shall discharge any debt contracted before the passage of the same.

EXPLANATION: This clause gives the CS Congress the authority to regulate immigration and bankruptcies—but these laws must be the same across all of the Southern states.

With this power Congress can provide citizenship for those who are qualified, while prohibiting citizenship for those who are not qualified. At the same time, through the issuance of fair laws regarding bankruptcy, the Confederate people are protected from indigence and poverty if they cannot pay their debts.

Finally, this clause orders that the CS Congress cannot make laws that allow it to avoid payment of its own debts.

ARTICLE 1, SECTION 8, CLAUSE 5

The Congress shall have power to coin money, regulate the value thereof, and of foreign coin, and fix the standard of weights and measures.

EXPLANATION: This clause gives the CS Congress the power to make metal and paper money, and to decide what its value should be. It is also in charge of the Confederacy's system of weights and measurements.

In both cases, however, there must be standardization, so that money, weights, and measurements are the same in every Confederate state.

ARTICLE 1, SECTION 8, CLAUSE 6

The Congress shall have power to provide for the punishment of counterfeiting the securities and current coin of the Confederate States.

EXPLANATION: In this clause the CS Congress is given the power to punish those who print fake money and government bonds.

ARTICLE 1, SECTION 8, CLAUSE 7

The Congress shall have power to establish post offices and post routes; but the expenses of the Post Office Department, after the 1st day of March in the year of our Lord eighteen hundred and sixty-three, shall be paid out of its own revenues.

EXPLANATION: In this clause Congress is empowered to create and operate a postal system across the Confederacy, including mail handling and establishing routes for mail delivery.

After March 1, 1863, however, the CS Post Office will no longer receive money from Congress, but must by then be financially self-sufficient.

ARTICLE 1, SECTION 8, CLAUSE 8

The Congress shall have power to promote the progress of science and useful arts, by securing for limited times to authors and inventors the exclusive right to their respective writings and discoveries.

EXPLANATION: Here Congress is given the power to promote both science and art, and to make laws that protect the work of scientists, authors, and inventors. In this way inventive and artistic people have motivation to explore and create things, not only for personal fame and gain, but also for the betterment of society.

ARTICLE 1, SECTION 8, CLAUSE 9

The Congress shall have power to constitute tribunals
inferior to the Supreme Court.

EXPLANATION: This clause gives the CS Congress the power to set up
a system of governmental courts that operate below the level of the
Supreme Court. An example would be the establishment of district
courts: lower (state) courts that serve specific areas throughout the
Confederate states.

ARTICLE 1, SECTION 8, CLAUSE 10

The Congress shall have power to define and punish piracies and felonies committed on the high seas, and offenses against the law of nations.

EXPLANATION: This clause allows the CS Congress to determine and punish crimes perpetrated outside Confederate territory, particularly at sea. It is also given the authority to handle problems that might arise between Confederate citizens and foreign countries. In essence, this clause helps protect ships that journey beyond CS territory, as well as CS citizens who travel abroad.

ARTICLE 1, SECTION 8, CLAUSE 11

The Congress shall have power to declare war, grant letters of marque and reprisal, and make rules concerning captures on land and water.

EXPLANATION: This all important clause states that only the CS Congress has the power to declare war on another nation. In case of hostilities, Congress is also given the authority to establish regulations regarding the capture of enemy property on both land and water.

ARTICLE 1, SECTION 8, CLAUSE 12

The Congress shall have power to raise and support armies; but no appropriation of money to that use shall be for a longer term than two years.

EXPLANATION: This far reaching clause gives the CS Congress the power to impose a draft on Confederate citizens, and force them into military service in time of need. Along with the ability to establish armies, Congress has the right to pay, outfit, and supply the soldiers of those forces with whatever it deems necessary. This would include, of course, a salary, food, clothing, and weaponry.

To keep the CS military in check and prevent the establishment of military rule, however, the CS Constitution here stipulates that Congress can only fund its armies for a period of two years. After that, the situation is reevaluated, and money can be appropriated for another two years if need be.

ARTICLE 1, SECTION 8, CLAUSE 13

The Congress shall have power to provide and maintain a navy.

EXPLANATION: This clause allows the CS Congress to set up and operate a national navy in order to protect the Confederacy's seas and coastline.

ARTICLE 1, SECTION 8, CLAUSE 14

The Congress shall have power to make rules for the government and regulation of the land and naval forces.

EXPLANATION: This clause allows Congress to create laws regarding the supervision of both the CS army and the CS navy.

ARTICLE 1, SECTION 8, CLAUSE 15

The Congress shall have power to provide for calling forth the militia to execute the laws of the Confederate States, suppress insurrections, and repel invasions.

EXPLANATION: This clause gives the CS Congress the authority to call up a military body in order to enforce Confederate law, quell riots, and defend against incursion by foreign nations.

ARTICLE 1, SECTION 8, CLAUSE 16

The Congress shall have power to provide for organizing, arming, and disciplining the militia, and for governing such part of them as may be employed in the service of the Confederate States; reserving to the States, respectively, the appointment of the officers, and the authority of training the militia according to the discipline prescribed by Congress.

EXPLANATION: Here the CS Congress is imbued with the authority to establish, organize, arm, train, and control the Confederate military. The individual Confederate states, however, are given the power to select their own officers and train their own armies, as long as this is done according to the rules laid out by Congress.

ARTICLE 1, SECTION 8, CLAUSE 17

The Congress shall have power to exercise exclusive legislation, in all cases whatsoever, over such district (not exceeding ten miles square) as may, by cession of one or more States and the acceptance of Congress, become the seat of the Government of the Confederate States; and to exercise like authority over all places purchased by the consent of the Legislature of the State in which the same shall be, for the erection of forts, magazines, arsenals, dockyards, and other needful buildings; and

EXPLANATION: This clause gives the CS Congress the power to accept land that is voluntarily given to them by the states to use as the site for the Confederate Capitol.[9] The property in question cannot be more than ten square miles in size.

Congress is also given exclusive control of the district in which the Confederate Capitol is situated, along with any other properties that are bought from willing Confederates states. On these sites Congress is allowed to build any type of structure it sees fit, including military fortifications, shipyards, and docks.

---

9. The first Confederate Capitol, established in February 1861, was at Montgomery, Alabama. In the Summer of 1861 this was relocated to the larger city of Richmond, Virginia. A third temporary Confederate capitol was set up in early April 1865 at Danville, Virginia, just prior to General Robert E. Lee's surrender.

ARTICLE 1, SECTION 8, CLAUSE 18

The Congress shall have power to make all laws which shall be necessary and proper for carrying into execution the foregoing powers, and all other powers vested by this Constitution in the Government of the Confederate States, or in any department or officer thereof.

EXPLANATION: This clause gives the CS Congress extreme flexibility in creating any laws it regards as "necessary and proper" in order to carry out the many congressional powers and responsibilities that are enumerated in Section 8 of the CS Constitution. This wide ranging authority extends to any governmental department or officer as well.

ARTICLE 1, SECTION 9, CLAUSE 1

The importation of negroes of the African race from any foreign country other than the slaveholding States or Territories of the United States of America, is hereby forbidden; and Congress is required to pass such laws as shall effectually prevent the same.

EXPLANATION: Section 9 deals chiefly with the limitations imposed on the powers of the CS Congress. Beginning with this clause, it permanently bans the foreign slave trade across the CSA. However, it permits slave trading with the USA and with the Western Territories (that is, those regions that would one day become the Western states).

ARTICLE 1, SECTION 9, CLAUSE 2

Congress shall also have power to prohibit the introduction of slaves from any State not a member of, or Territory not belonging to, this Confederacy.

EXPLANATION: While Clause 1 bans the foreign slave trade, this clause goes a step further by giving the CS Congress the power to prohibit trade with any US state or any non-Confederate region of the Western Territories that it chooses.

ARTICLE 1, SECTION 9, CLAUSE 3

The privilege of the writ of habeas corpus shall not be suspended, unless when in cases of rebellion or invasion the public safety may require it.

EXPLANATION: This clause stipulates that the writ of *habeas corpus* (that is, the right of a citizen to be brought before a judge and formally charged with a crime before being put in jail) cannot be suspended by the CS government.

However, this clause provides several exceptions to this rule: the government may suspend *habeas corpus* during subversive revolts, foreign intrusion into CS territory, and in any situation where the public safety is considered to be in peril.

ARTICLE 1, SECTION 9, CLAUSE 4

No bill of attainder, ex post facto law, or law denying or impairing the right of property in negro slaves shall be passed.

EXPLANATION: This three-part clause states that the CS government cannot create:

1) A bill of attainder. (A bill of attainder is a law allowing an individual to be convicted without a trial.)

2) An *ex post facto* law. (An *ex post facto* law is one that allows an individual to be punished for a crime retroactively; that is, for a deed that was not considered a crime at the time he or she committed it.)

3) A law prohibiting the right to own slaves. (This stipulation was important because the Confederacy had not yet figured out how to end slavery without hurting both slaves and their owners. This commonsense view was later completely ignored by US President Abraham Lincoln, for he hoped—without success, as it would turn out—that emancipation would hurt the Southern economy, initiate slave revolts, drain Confederate military strength, and start a race war across Dixie. In short, as the American Abolition Movement began in the South, and as the South had been trying to ban slavery since the creation of the US in 1776, this particular provision was considered temporary until a safe and rational method of Southern emancipation could be worked out.)

ARTICLE 1, SECTION 9, CLAUSE 5

No capitation or other direct tax shall be laid, unless in proportion to the census or enumeration hereinbefore directed to be taken.

EXPLANATION: This clause is essentially a restatement of Article 1, Section 2, Clause 3, which declares that the CS Congress cannot lay a direct tax on Confederate citizens (only an indirect tax). Additionally, a direct tax must be levied on a state according to its population.

ARTICLE 1, SECTION 9, CLAUSE 6

No tax or duty shall be laid on articles exported from any State, except by a vote of two-thirds of both Houses.

EXPLANATION: This clause orders that the CS Congress cannot place a tax or tariff on state exports, unless two-thirds of both the Senate and the House of Representatives vote to do so.

ARTICLE 1, SECTION 9, CLAUSE 7

No preference shall be given by any regulation of commerce or revenue to the ports of one State over those of another.

EXPLANATION: This clause declares that the CS Congress cannot give commercial or economic advantage to one Confederate seaport over another, which allows all of the Confederate states the opportunity to prosper equally. (However, it can require the Confederate states to tax ships from other Confederate states when entering their ports.)

ARTICLE 1, SECTION 9, CLAUSE 8

No money shall be drawn from the Treasury, but in consequence of appropriations made by law; and a regular statement and account of the receipts and expenditures of all public money shall be published from time to time.

EXPLANATION: In this clause the CS Congress is only allowed to withdraw money from the CS Treasury according to the law (known as "appropriation bills"). In addition, an accurate report of what money Congress takes and how it is used must be published and made available to taxpayers on a regular basis.

ARTICLE 1, SECTION 9, CLAUSE 9

Congress shall appropriate no money from the Treasury except by a vote of two-thirds of both Houses, taken by yeas and nays, unless it be asked and estimated for by some one of the heads of departments and submitted to Congress by the President; or for the purpose of paying its own expenses and contingencies; or for the payment of claims against the Confederate States, the justice of which shall have been judicially declared by a tribunal for the investigation of claims against the Government, which it is hereby made the duty of Congress to establish.

EXPLANATION: This clause places rigorous fiscal responsibility upon the CS Congress by stating that:

1) Congress can only take money from the CS Treasury with a "yea" and "nay" vote of two-thirds in both the Senate and the House of Representatives, or by request of the CS president.

2) Congress can take money from the CS Treasury to pay for its own expenses.

3) Congress can take money from the CS Treasury to pay for "claims" against the CS government, such as the national debt.

4) Congress must set up a court to examine any claims made against the CS government.

ARTICLE 1, SECTION 9, CLAUSE 10

All bills appropriating money shall specify in Federal currency the exact amount of each appropriation and the purposes for which it is made; and Congress shall grant no extra compensation to any public contractor, officer, agent, or servant, after such contract shall have been made or such service rendered.

EXPLANATION: According to this fiscally responsible clause, the CS Congress cannot take money from the CS Treasury unless an exact amount is specified. And after an appropriation bill is passed, Congress cannot add even a single penny to the sum requested.

ARTICLE 1, SECTION 9, CLAUSE 11

No title of nobility shall be granted by the Confederate States; and no person holding any office of profit or trust under them shall, without the consent of the Congress, accept of any present, emolument, office, or title of any kind whatever, from any king, prince, or foreign state.

EXPLANATION: In this clause, known as the "Title of Nobility Clause," the Confederate government is prohibited from creating or handing out titles of nobility (an aristocratic class possessing hereditary entitlement).

Additionally, no CS government worker, in particular government officials, are allowed to receive gifts, money, jobs, or titles from a royal or from a foreign nation. (Note: private Confederate citizens are exempt from these rules.)

ARTICLE 1, SECTION 9, CLAUSE 12

Congress shall make no law respecting an establishment of religion, or prohibiting the free exercise thereof; or abridging the freedom of speech, or of the press; or the right of the people peaceably to assemble and petition the Government for a redress of grievances.

EXPLANATION: With this clause the CSA begins incorporating the first ten amendments to the US Constitution, known as the "Bill of Rights," directly into its Constitution. This clause, the First Amendment, contains five important stipulations:

1) The CS Congress cannot make a law creating a religion.

2) The CS Congress cannot interfere with one's right to practice his or her religion.

3) The CS Congress cannot interfere with an individual's freedom of expression.

4) The CS Congress cannot tell the press what it can and cannot say.

5) The CS Congress cannot prevent people from gathering peacefully.

6) The CS Congress cannot prevent CS citizens from complaining to the government over perceived abuses.

ARTICLE 1, SECTION 9, CLAUSE 13

A well-regulated militia being necessary to the security of a free State, the right of the people to keep and bear arms shall not be infringed.

EXPLANATION: This clause, the Second Amendment (of the Bill of Rights) to the US Constitution, states that the citizens of the CSA have the right to own and carry weapons, and that the CS government has no authority to interfere with this right.

While the CS wording here is exactly the same as in the US Constitution, the US version is punctuated differently: in the Bill of Rights there is a comma after the word "militia."

Anti-South and anti-gun proponents have long used this minor grammatical variation to try and prove that the US Founding Fathers originally intended that the right to carry guns belongs only to government-approved military groups. However, both the CS version and the US version literally state that it is "the right of *the people* to keep and bear arms." The intended meaning of the CS and the US Founding Fathers is thus patently clear, invalidating all arguments to the contrary.

ARTICLE 1, SECTION 9, CLAUSE 14

No soldier shall, in time of peace, be quartered in any
house without the consent of the owner; nor in time of
war, but in a manner to be prescribed by law.

EXPLANATION: According to this clause, the Third Amendment (of
the Bill of Rights) to the US Constitution, the CS government cannot
force its citizens, in time of peace or war, to allow soldiers to stay in
their homes without their express consent. However, during time of
war an exception may be made to this rule—if an extreme situation
warrants it.

ARTICLE 1, SECTION 9, CLAUSE 15

The right of the people to be secure in their persons, houses, papers, and effects, against unreasonable searches and seizures, shall not be violated; and no warrants shall issue but upon probable cause, supported by oath or affirmation, and particularly describing the place to be searched and the persons or things to be seized.

EXPLANATION: This clause, the Fourth Amendment (of the Bill of Rights) to the US Constitution, guarantees that Confederate citizens have the right to feel safe and secure in their homes against government intrusion.

Furthermore, the CS government cannot enter a person's home without probable cause (that is, the police believe he or she has committed a crime) and a search warrant (a document issued by a judge allowing the police to legally enter someone's property).

Lastly, all search warrants must identify the place that is to be searched, the individual who is to be arrested, and the items that are later seized and removed from the property.

ARTICLE 1, SECTION 9, CLAUSE 16

> No person shall be held to answer for a capital or otherwise infamous crime, unless on a presentment or indictment of a grand jury, except in cases arising in the land or naval forces, or in the militia, when in actual service in time of war or public danger; nor shall any person be subject for the same offense to be twice put in jeopardy of life or limb; nor be compelled, in any criminal case, to be a witness against himself; nor be deprived of life, liberty, or property without due process of law; nor shall private property be taken for public use, without just compensation.

EXPLANATION: This clause, the Fifth Amendment (of the Bill of Rights) to the US Constitution, along with the next clause, Clause 17, concern criminal law (as opposed to common law). Here Clause 16 states that:

1) A Confederate citizen accused of a serious ("capital") crime or a very bad ("infamous") crime cannot be put on trial without first being brought before a grand jury, whose role is to decide if the charges are substantial enough to justify a trial. Exceptions to this rule include cases involving the military.

2) The CS government cannot try a Confederate citizen for the same crime twice.

3) The CS government cannot force a Confederate citizen who is on trial to say anything that might damage his or her case.

4) The CS government cannot imprison or execute someone, or seize one's property, without a fair, judicious, and lawful trial.

5) The CS government cannot take an individual's private property for public use without paying the owner a fair price in return.

ARTICLE 1, SECTION 9, CLAUSE 17

> In all criminal prosecutions the accused shall enjoy the right to a speedy and public trial, by an impartial jury of the State and district wherein the crime shall have been committed, which district shall have been previously ascertained by law, and to be informed of the nature and cause of the accusation; to be confronted with the witnesses against him; to have compulsory process for obtaining witnesses in his favor; and to have the assistance of counsel for his defense.

EXPLANATION: This clause, the Sixth Amendment (of the Bill of Rights) to the US Constitution, states that a Confederate citizen who is arrested has a right to:

1) A trial that will be held as soon as possible in a public court of law.

2) An impartial jury of his peers who live in the area where the crime is alleged to have been committed.

3) Be told in detail what crime he is being accused of so that he can prepare the proper defense.

4) Appear in person in court in order to face his accusers.

5) Call witnesses favoring the accused to testify in his defense, selection of whom will be performed by the CS government if necessary.

6) Have an attorney represent him, funded by the CS government if need be.

ARTICLE 1, SECTION 9, CLAUSE 18

In suits at common law, where the value in controversy shall exceed twenty dollars, the right of trial by jury shall be preserved; and no fact so tried by a jury shall be otherwise reexamined in any court of the Confederacy, than according to the rules of common law.

EXPLANATION: With this clause, the Seventh Amendment (of the Bill of Rights) to the US Constitution, we turn from the topic of criminal law (Clauses 16 and 17) to common law, wherein disputes between individuals are settled in a court and tried by a jury (known as a "civil trial").

Here, the CS Constitution gives Confederate citizens the right to bring civil cases to trial—though a trial is not necessary if the dispute concerns an issue that is worth less than $20.00 (the equivalent of about $500.00 today).

In addition, if a civil case is appealed and ends up in a higher court, the new judge is not permitted to challenge the facts of the previous trial. However, according to CS common law, if he decides that the laws were misinterpreted, or that the evidence presented in the first trial was insufficient, he may alter the verdict.

ARTICLE 1, SECTION 9, CLAUSE 19

Excessive bail shall not be required, nor excessive fines imposed, nor cruel and unusual punishments inflicted.

EXPLANATION: This clause, the Eighth Amendment (of the Bill of Rights) to the US Constitution, prohibits judges from imposing unreasonable bail or fines on individuals brought before them in a court of law. It also prohibits savage or uncommon penalties from being inflicted upon the accused or the convicted.

ARTICLE 1, SECTION 9, CLAUSE 20

Every law, or resolution having the force of law, shall relate to but one subject, and that shall be expressed in the title.

EXPLANATION: This clause limits bills moving through Congress to a single topic. This is the Confederacy's attempt to prevent congressmen from attaching countless "riders" to their bills.

A rider is a clause or provision added to a bill that has little or no connection to the subject of that bill. Since it would probably not pass if submitted by itself, it is attached to a bill that probably will, a shrewd and underhanded tactic often used to push through unpopular or controversial provisions. (Note: the US Constitution does not prohibit riders.)

ARTICLE 1, SECTION 10, CLAUSE 1

No State shall enter into any treaty, alliance, or confederation; grant letters of marque and reprisal; coin money; make anything but gold and silver coin a tender in payment of debts; pass any bill of attainder, or ex post facto law, or law impairing the obligation of contracts; or grant any title of nobility.

EXPLANATION: With Section 10 we begin a list of the limitations on the powers of the Confederate states. In Clause 1, known as the "Contract Clause," Confederate states are banned from exercising powers that have been given to the central government, or from assuming powers that the states were never intended to have.

Prohibited powers to the states are: entering into treaties, alliances, or confederations (that is, agreements or relationships with other states or nations); issuing letters of marque and reprisal (a government license allowing a private citizen to capture enemy vessels and have them brought before a naval court); and coining and printing money (though the states are allowed to coin gold and silver money to pay their debts with).

The Confederate states are also prohibited from: issuing bills of attainder (a law permitting someone to be convicted without a trial) or an *ex post facto* law (a provision that allows a person to be punished for a crime that was not considered a crime at the time it was perpetrated); creating laws that interfere with contractual agreements (compacts between two or more private parties); and handing out titles of nobility (a class of individuals who, either by birth or honorary rank, possess privileges not given to other members of society, such as kings and queens, princes and princesses, dukes and duchesses, barons and baronesses, and counts and countesses).

ARTICLE 1, SECTION 10, CLAUSE 2

No State shall, without the consent of the Congress, lay any imposts or duties on imports or exports, except what may be absolutely necessary for executing its inspection laws; and the net produce of all duties and imposts, laid by any State on imports, or exports, shall be for the use of the Treasury of the Confederate States; and all such laws shall be subject to the revision and control of Congress.

EXPLANATION: In this clause Confederate states are not allowed to impose taxes on foreign imports and exports, unless they have the authorization of the CS Congress. The states, however, may levy a small charge to help pay for the costs of inspecting goods that cross their borders.

Furthermore, when a state tax is placed upon an import or export, the money resulting from that tariff goes to the CS Treasury.

Finally, these laws are to be under the control of the CS Congress, and may be changed at any time by that body.

ARTICLE 1, SECTION 10, CLAUSE 3

No State shall, without the consent of Congress, lay any duty on tonnage, except on seagoing vessels, for the improvement of its rivers and harbors navigated by the said vessels; but such duties shall not conflict with any treaties of the Confederate States with foreign nations; and any surplus revenue thus derived shall, after making such improvement, be paid into the common treasury. Nor shall any State keep troops or ships of war in time of peace, enter into any agreement or compact with another State, or with a foreign power, or engage in war, unless actually invaded, or in such imminent danger as will not admit of delay. But when any river divides or flows through two or more States they may enter into compacts with each other to improve the navigation thereof.

EXPLANATION: In this clause the Confederate states are banned from imposing taxes on ships according to their weight, unless they are authorized to do so by the CS Congress. The states can, however, issue taxes on seagoing vessels, the money from which is to be used to improve the waterways upon which such ships travel. In such cases the state tax cannot interfere with government agreements with foreign countries, and any extra money earned through such means must go into the CS Treasury.

Here the Confederate states are also forbidden from possessing soldiers and ships, forging treaties with other Confederate states or foreign nations, and starting or fighting wars—unless their state is invaded and there is no time to get congressional approval.

Finally, if a river splits or travels through two or more states, those states are permitted to forge alliances with one another in order to improve the navigation of that waterway.

President of the Confederate States of America, Jefferson Davis.

Article 2

Executive Branch

ARTICLE 2, SECTION 1, CLAUSE 1

The executive power shall be vested in a President of the Confederate States of America. He and the Vice President shall hold their offices for the term of six years; but the President shall not be reeligible. The President and Vice President shall be elected as follows:

EXPLANATION: With Article 2 we have the establishment of the second branch of the CS government: the executive branch, in charge of enforcing the laws created and passed by the CS Congress (and which will later be interpreted by the judicial branch).

Clause 1 stipulates that the head of the executive branch is the CS president, who is allowed to serve only one six-year term. The CS vice president also serves a six-year term—though he is permitted to be reelected.

ARTICLE 2, SECTION 1, CLAUSE 2

Each State shall appoint, in such manner as the Legislature thereof may direct, a number of electors equal to the whole number of Senators and Representatives to which the State may be entitled in the Congress; but no Senator or Representative or person holding an office of trust or profit under the Confederate States shall be appointed an elector.

EXPLANATION: This clause establishes the CS Electoral College. In order to fairly elect a CS president and a CS vice president, it orders the Confederate states to appoint, according to instructions created by the legislative branch, individuals known as "electors." The number of electors must match the number of senators and representatives in Congress.

Senators and representatives, along with high-ranking CS officials in positions of "trust or profit," however, are not permitted to become electors.[10]

---

10. Typically, electors are selected from among party activists, party leaders, elected state officials, and those who have personal or political connections to the candidates.

ARTICLE 2, SECTION 1, CLAUSE 3

The electors shall meet in their respective States and vote by ballot for President and Vice President, one of whom, at least, shall not be an inhabitant of the same State with themselves; they shall name in their ballots the person voted for as President, and in distinct ballots the person voted for as Vice President, and they shall make distinct lists of all persons voted for as President, and of all persons voted for as Vice President, and of the number of votes for each, which lists they shall sign and certify, and transmit, sealed, to the seat of the Government of the Confederate States, directed to the President of the Senate; the President of the Senate shall, in the presence of the Senate and House of Representatives, open all the certificates, and the votes shall then be counted; the person having the greatest number of votes for President shall be the President, if such number be a majority of the whole number of electors appointed; and if no person have such majority, then from the persons having the highest numbers, not exceeding three, on the list of those voted for as President, the House of Representatives shall choose immediately, by ballot, the President. But in choosing the President the votes shall be taken by States, the representation from each State having one vote; a quorum for this purpose shall consist of a member or members from two-thirds of the States, and a majority of all the States shall be necessary to a choice. And if the House of Representatives shall not choose a President, whenever the right of choice shall devolve upon them, before the 4th day of March next following, then the Vice President shall act as President, as in case of the death, or other constitutional disability of the President.

EXPLANATION: This clause, in a slightly different form, was originally part of Article 2, Section 1, Clause 3, of the US Constitution. The United States later adopted it (in 1804) as the Twelfth Amendment. In the CS Constitution of 1861, however, it remained Article 2, Section 1, Clause 3.[11]

This clause, Clause 3, deals with the Electoral College and the election of the CS president. It orders that electors meet, not as one body, but rather in their own states, where they are to vote for the president and vice president on separate ballots. A report of the names of all those who vote, along with the totals from each state, are to be prepared and submitted to the president of the Senate. He is to open the report in full view of both Houses, after which the votes are to be counted.

The candidate with the highest number of total electoral votes becomes president. If no one has a majority, then the House of Representatives vote by ballot from among the top three vote-getting candidates, "a majority of all the states" being necessary to make the final decision. If the House of Representatives does not cast its vote by the following March 4, then the vice president "shall act as president."

11. Note that the original US Article 2, Section 1, Clause 3, was divided into three smaller clauses by the CSA, and are known in the CS Constitution as Article 2, Section 1, Clauses 3, 4, and 5.

ARTICLE 2, SECTION 1, CLAUSE 4

The person having the greatest number of votes as Vice President shall be the Vice President, if such number be a majority of the whole number of electors appointed; and if no person have a majority, then, from the two highest numbers on the list, the Senate shall choose the Vice President; a quorum for the purpose shall consist of two-thirds of the whole number of Senators, and a majority of the whole number shall be necessary to a choice.

EXPLANATION: This clause, part of the Twelfth Amendment of the US Constitution, deals with the CS Electoral College and the election of the CS vice president.

It orders that the candidate with the most electoral votes becomes the vice president. However, if no one has a majority, the Senate is to vote between the two candidates with the most votes. At least two-thirds of the Senate must participate. The candidate with the most votes from this group becomes vice president.

ARTICLE 2, SECTION 1, CLAUSE 5

But no person constitutionally ineligible to the office of
President shall be eligible to that of Vice President of
the Confederate States.

EXPLANATION: This clause, part of the Twelfth Amendment of the US
Constitution, deals with the eligibility of those who would become the
CS vice president.

While it forbids anyone who is "constitutionally ineligible" from
serving in that office, the CS Constitution does not define this term.
However, it does state, if obliquely, that the CS vice president should
possess the same qualifications as the CS president.[12]

---

12. See Article 2, Section 1, Clause 7.

ARTICLE 2, SECTION 1, CLAUSE 6

The Congress may determine the time of choosing the electors, and the day on which they shall give their votes; which day shall be the same throughout the Confederate States.

EXPLANATION: This clause stipulates that only Congress has the authority to set the date for selecting electors, as well as the day upon which they cast their votes for the CS president and the CS vice president. Additionally, voting day must be held on the same day in all of the Confederate states.

ARTICLE 2, SECTION 1, CLAUSE 7

No person except a natural-born citizen of the Confederate States, or a citizen thereof at the time of the adoption of this Constitution, or a citizen thereof born in the United States prior to the 20th of December, 1860, shall be eligible to the office of President; neither shall any person be eligible to that office who shall not have attained the age of thirty-five years, and been fourteen years a resident within the limits of the Confederate States, as they may exist at the time of his election.

EXPLANATION: This clause lays out the requirements for the CS president:

1) He must have been born in one of the Confederate states; or have been a citizen of one of the Confederate states at the time of the ratification of the CS Constitution; or he must have been born in the US prior to the secession of the first Southern state (South Carolina) on December 20, 1860.

2) He must be at least thirty-five years old.

3) He must be a resident of the CSA at the time of his election.

ARTICLE 2, SECTION 1, CLAUSE 8

In case of the removal of the President from office, or of his death, resignation, or inability to discharge the powers and duties of said office, the same shall devolve on the Vice President; and the Congress may, by law, provide for the case of removal, death, resignation, or inability, both of the President and Vice President, declaring what officer shall then act as President; and such officer shall act accordingly until the disability be removed or a President shall be elected.

EXPLANATION: This clause stipulates that in case the CS president is removed from office, dies while in office, resigns, or in any way is unable to fulfill his duties, the vice president becomes president.

In case the vice president is also either removed from office, dies while in office, resigns, or in any way is unable to fulfill his duties, the CS Congress has the authority to replace both positions with whomever they see fit. The selected individuals must behave lawfully while serving as president and vice president, until their positions are officially filled again at election time.

ARTICLE 2, SECTION 1, CLAUSE 9

The President shall, at stated times, receive for his services a compensation, which shall neither be increased nor diminished during the period for which he shall have been elected; and he shall not receive within that period any other emolument from the Confederate States, or any of them.

EXPLANATION: This clause permits the CS president to have a salary and to have his expenses paid for by Congress. His salary cannot be increased or decreased during his tenure (preventing undue influence by congressmen).

Finally, as a further anti-corruption measure, he is not allowed any other type of compensation, either from the CS government or from the individual Confederate states.

ARTICLE 2, SECTION 1, CLAUSE 10

Before he enters on the execution of the duties of his office he shall take the following oath or affirmation:

> I do solemnly swear (or affirm) that I will faithfully execute the office of President of the Confederate States, and will, to the best of my ability, preserve, protect, and defend the Constitution thereof.

EXPLANATION: Prior to taking office, the CS president must profess the above public declaration, promising to do his best to fulfill his duties, while preserving, protecting, and defending the CS Constitution. Technically speaking, it is only after taking this oath that he becomes president.

ARTICLE 2, SECTION 2, CLAUSE 1

The President shall be Commander-in-Chief of the Army and Navy of the Confederate States, and of the militia of the several States, when called into the actual service of the Confederate States; he may require the opinion, in writing, of the principal officer in each of the Executive Departments, upon any subject relating to the duties of their respective offices; and he shall have power to grant reprieves and pardons for offenses against the Confederate States, except in cases of impeachment.

EXPLANATION: In this clause the duties and powers of the CS president are established. He is given the position of commander-in-chief over both the CS army and the CS navy. As head of the CS military he has the authority to seek advice from his cabinet (the "principal officers of the Executive Departments"). Finally, the president can grant pardons and reprieves for crimes against the Confederate States, except for cases in which a public official is charged with a crime.

This ingenious clause helps protect the Confederacy against the formation of a military dictatorship by putting an elected civilian in charge of the CS armed forces, one who is susceptible to impeachment or being voted out of office by the people if he abuses his position.

ARTICLE 2, SECTION 2, CLAUSE 2

He shall have power, by and with the advice and consent of the Senate, to make treaties; provided two-thirds of the Senators present concur; and he shall nominate, and by and with the advice and consent of the Senate shall appoint, ambassadors, other public ministers and consuls, judges of the Supreme Court, and all other officers of the Confederate States whose appointments are not herein otherwise provided for, and which shall be established by law; but the Congress may, by law, vest the appointment of such inferior officers, as they think proper, in the President alone, in the courts of law, or in the heads of departments.

EXPLANATION: This clause gives the CS president several wide-ranging powers. He not only has the authority to make agreements with foreign nations, but he may also appoint important government positions, such as diplomats, supervisors, administrators, Supreme Court justices, and any other significant officer of the Confederate States he chooses—as long as two-thirds of the members of the Senate agree with his decisions.

On the other hand, Congress has the right to give the president the power to select lower level officials ("inferior officers") as he sees fit, without congressional approval.

ARTICLE 2, SECTION 2, CLAUSE 3

The principal officer in each of the Executive Departments, and all persons connected with the diplomatic service, may be removed from office at the pleasure of the President. All other civil officers of the Executive Departments may be removed at any time by the President, or other appointing power, when their services are unnecessary, or for dishonesty, incapacity, inefficiency, misconduct, or neglect of duty; and when so removed, the removal shall be reported to the Senate, together with the reasons therefor.

EXPLANATION: This clause allows the CS president the authority to terminate anyone working in the executive branch of the government, along with those serving in the diplomatic service. Reasons for dismissal can include nonessential positions, lying, illness, lack of ability, mismanagement, and in general failing to perform one's duties. Upon firing an individual, the president must send a report to the CS Senate explaining the reasons for his actions.

ARTICLE 2, SECTION 2, CLAUSE 4

The President shall have power to fill all vacancies that may happen during the recess of the Senate, by granting commissions which shall expire at the end of their next session; but no person rejected by the Senate shall be reappointed to the same office during their ensuing recess.

EXPLANATION: In this clause the CS president is authorized to appoint someone to fill a vacancy that occurs while Congress is on vacation, an appointment referred to as *ad interim* (Latin: "for the interval," that is, temporarily). Such appointments, however, run out at the close of the following session (though the individual may be voted back in by Congress if that body so desires).

Finally, the president may not reappoint someone to an office he has held before if that person has already been ousted by the Senate.

ARTICLE 2, SECTION 3, CLAUSE 1

The President shall, from time to time, give to the Congress information of the state of the Confederacy, and recommend to their consideration such measures as he shall judge necessary and expedient; he may, on extraordinary occasions, convene both Houses, or either of them; and in case of disagreement between them, with respect to the time of adjournment, he may adjourn them to such time as he shall think proper; he shall receive ambassadors and other public ministers; he shall take care that the laws be faithfully executed, and shall commission all the officers of the Confederate States.

EXPLANATION: In this clause the CS president is given more duties and powers.

He must occasionally report to Congress concerning the condition of the Confederacy, and offer suggestions on topics and issues he considers vital to improving the country. On "extraordinary occasions" he can assemble one or both Houses of Congress, and close them down as he sees fit.

The CS president must also meet with diplomats and other public officials, be sure that the laws of the Confederacy are "faithfully executed," and oversee the appointment of all important government officials.

ARTICLE 2, SECTION 4, CLAUSE 1

The President, Vice President, and all civil officers of the Confederate States, shall be removed from office on impeachment for and conviction of treason, bribery, or other high crimes and misdemeanors.

EXPLANATION: This clause stipulates that the CS president, the CS vice president, and all other officers of the CS government, are subject to criminal charges and removal from office for the following offenses:

1) Making war against the Confederate States (treason).

2) Exchanging money or gifts for influence and advantage (bribery).

3) Any other illicit behaviors or activities that may show an individual is not morally qualified to hold his position.

Vice President of the Confederate States of America, Alexander Hamilton Stephens.

Article 3

Judicial Branch

ARTICLE 3, SECTION 1, CLAUSE 1

The judicial power of the Confederate States shall be vested in one Supreme Court, and in such inferior courts as the Congress may, from time to time, ordain and establish. The judges, both of the Supreme and inferior courts, shall hold their offices during good behavior, and shall, at stated times, receive for their services a compensation which shall not be diminished during their continuance in office.

EXPLANATION: With Article 3 the CS Constitution establishes the third and final branch of the CS government: the judicial branch, which interprets the laws created by Congress and which are approved by the president.

Clause 1 begins by setting up a system of national courts by placing the judicial power of the Confederacy in a single Supreme Court, and also in lower courts that are created by the CS Congress.

Supreme Court judges, as well as judges of the lower federal courts, are promised long lasting jobs, and are authorized to be paid a salary by the CS government—as long as they fulfill the duties of their positions properly.

ARTICLE 3, SECTION 2, CLAUSE 1

The judicial power shall extend to all cases arising under this Constitution, the laws of the Confederate States, and treaties made, or which shall be made, under their authority; to all cases affecting ambassadors, other public ministers and consuls; to all cases of admiralty and maritime jurisdiction; to controversies to which the Confederate States shall be a party; to controversies between two or more States; between a State and citizens of another State, where the State is plaintiff; between citizens claiming lands under grants of different States; and between a State or the citizens thereof, and foreign states, citizens, or subjects; but no State shall be sued by a citizen or subject of any foreign state.

EXPLANATION: This clause, based on the Eleventh Amendment of the US Constitution, sets up the legal jurisdiction of the CS government and the Confederate states.

It declares that the authority of the judicial branch will encompass all cases involving the CS Constitution, the laws of the CS government, foreign agreements, diplomats, foreign ministers, the naval department, marine territories, lawsuits by citizens against the Confederate states, lawsuits by the Confederate states against citizens, disputes between two or more states, disagreements involving land grants in different states, foreigners, foreign states, and foreign subjects. Foreigners, however, are not allowed to sue a Confederate state.

ARTICLE 3, SECTION 2, CLAUSE 2

In all cases affecting ambassadors, other public ministers and consuls, and those in which a State shall be a party, the Supreme Court shall have original jurisdiction. In all the other cases before mentioned, the Supreme Court shall have appellate jurisdiction both as to law and fact, with such exceptions and under such regulations as the Congress shall make.

EXPLANATION: This clause specifies that only the CS Supreme Court has jurisdiction over cases involving diplomats, foreign dignitaries, and the Confederate states. The term "original jurisdiction" here refers to the right and authority of the Supreme Court to hear such cases first, before any other court.

Cases involving issues, organizations, or individuals not named above are relegated to the lower state courts, known as "district courts." If a decision made in a district court is appealed, it can go to the Supreme Court for review, where, after thoroughly examining the case, it has the authority to reverse the decision if deemed necessary. This right, the Supreme Court's power to review and alter rulings, is referred to as "appellate jurisdiction."

ARTICLE 3, SECTION 2, CLAUSE 3

The trial of all crimes, except in cases of impeachment, shall be by jury, and such trial shall be held in the State where the said crimes shall have been committed; but when not committed within any State, the trial shall be at such place or places as the Congress may by law have directed.

EXPLANATION: This clause instructs that all criminal trials—except for cases in which government officials are charged with misconduct—will be determined by a jury in the Confederate state where the crime is alleged to have been perpetrated. If a crime is committed outside the Confederate states, the CS Congress has the power to decide when and where the trial will be held.

The purpose of jury trials, of course, is to protect the accused from the random opinions, judgements, and decisions of court officials, making this clause an especially important part of the CS Constitution.

ARTICLE 3, SECTION 3, CLAUSE 1

Treason against the Confederate States shall consist only in levying war against them, or in adhering to their enemies, giving them aid and comfort. No person shall be convicted of treason unless on the testimony of two witnesses to the same overt act, or on confession in open court.

EXPLANATION: This clause clearly defines the word treason so that it cannot be used to arbitrarily punish those who merely disagree with the CS government (a custom popular with English kings, and some liberal US presidents, such as Abraham Lincoln).

Treason here is defined as waging war against the Confederate states, associating with enemies of the Confederate states, or giving assistance and moral support to such enemies.

Additionally, an individual cannot be convicted of the crime of treason unless there are two eyewitnesses, or the accused confesses in a public court of law.

ARTICLE 3, SECTION 3, CLAUSE 2

The Congress shall have power to declare the punishment of treason; but no attainder of treason shall work corruption of blood, or forfeiture, except during the life of the person attainted.

EXPLANATION: This clause states that the CS Congress has the authority to decide the punishment for treason, but, in order to protect those not directly involved, Congress may not impose penalties on the convicted person's relatives or descendants, or seize his property. Finally (as a reenforcement of the first provision), punishment for treason is only permitted while the convicted is alive—not after death.

Article 4

Confederate States

ARTICLE 4, SECTION 1, CLAUSE 1

Full faith and credit shall be given in each State to the public acts, records, and judicial proceedings of every other State; and the Congress may, by general laws, prescribe the manner in which such acts, records, and proceedings shall be proved, and the effect thereof.

EXPLANATION: With Article 4 the CS Constitution establishes the powers and roles of the individual Confederate states.

Beginning with Clause 1, it is ordered that the laws of each Confederate state will be recognized in all the others. In other words, to avoid inefficiency and confusion, the legal rights of an individual from one state are to be recognized in every state.

ARTICLE 4, SECTION 2, CLAUSE 1

The citizens of each State shall be entitled to all the privileges and immunities of citizens in the several States; and shall have the right of transit and sojourn in any State of this Confederacy, with their slaves and other property; and the right of property in said slaves shall not be thereby impaired.

EXPLANATION: This nationalistic clause stipulates that a Confederate citizen of one state may travel through, work in, or move to any other Confederate state, knowing that he will be legally protected and treated fairly as a member of the Confederate States of America, rather than just as a citizen from a different state.

Additionally, because the Confederacy had not yet figured out how to free its slaves without harming both the slaves and their owners, the CS government is not allowed to interfere with the travel or transport of servants throughout the Confederate states, nor is it allowed to hinder the right of one to own servants.[13]

---

13. Since tens of thousands of Southern blacks and Indians also owned black slaves (and even white slaves), this provision applies to *all* races, and is therefore nonracial.

ARTICLE 4, SECTION 2, CLAUSE 2

A person charged in any State with treason, felony, or other crime against the laws of such State, who shall flee from justice, and be found in another State, shall, on demand of the executive authority of the State from which he fled, be delivered up, to be removed to the State having jurisdiction of the crime.

EXPLANATION: This clause specifies that if a person perpetrates a crime (such as treason, or any other type of felony) and flees to another state, the governor of the state where the crime was committed can request that the criminal be extradited, that is, returned. Here, the CS Constitution prevents suspects and criminals from crossing state lines to escape punishment.

ARTICLE 4, SECTION 2, CLAUSE 3

No slave or other person held to service or labor in any State or Territory of the Confederate States, under the laws thereof, escaping or lawfully carried into another, shall, in consequence of any law or regulation therein, be discharged from such service or labor; but shall be delivered up on claim of the party to whom such slave belongs, or to whom such service or labor may be due.

EXPLANATION: This clause, known as the "Fugitive Slave Law," specifies that even if a slave flees or is legally taken out of his home state and into another, he is still bound to the service of his original owner. Furthermore, if anyone captures a runaway slave, he is to be given back to the original owner. As servants were worth the modern equivalent of $50,000 each, this clause was important to the financial stability of Southern slave owners until a workable solution to the problem of emancipation could be found.

 Slaves from the more racially tolerant South benefitted from the Fugitive Slave Law as well, for if they fled North, they would be subjected to the Yankees' incredibly brutal "Black Codes." These harsh racist laws, which had been in place across the Northern states almost since American slavery first arose in Massachusetts in the early 1600s, were heavily reenforced during the Civil War by none other than President Abraham Lincoln, a lifelong member of the American Colonization Society,[14] a Northern founded white racist organization.[15]

---

14. The stated goal of the American Colonization Society was to make America "white from coast to coast."
15. It was our sixteenth US president who often referred to blacks using the "n" word," continually called them an "inferior race," refused to give them citizenship or the right to vote, and campaigned throughout his entire political career to have them "shipped back to Africa." This is why, after all, President Lincoln's Preliminary Emancipation Proclamation, issued on September 22, 1862, contained one of his famous clauses calling for black deportation. It is little wonder that Southern blacks preferred their warm Dixie homeland to life in the far more bigoted cold North. It was Lincoln, the leader of the Northern states, who, on July 17, 1858, told an audience at Springfield, Illinois: "What I would most desire would be the separation of the white and black races." For more on this topic, see my book *Abraham Lincoln: The Southern View*.

ARTICLE 4, SECTION 3, CLAUSE 1

Other States may be admitted into this Confederacy by a vote of two-thirds of the whole House of Representatives and two-thirds of the Senate, the Senate voting by States; but no new State shall be formed or erected within the jurisdiction of any other State, nor any State be formed by the junction of two or more States, or parts of States, without the consent of the Legislatures of the States concerned, as well as of the Congress.

EXPLANATION: Non-Confederate states may join the CSA, but only with a two-thirds vote of approval from both the CS House of Representatives and the CS Senate. However, for a new Confederate state to be created by splitting off from an existing Confederate state, or from combining two or more existing Confederate states, the approval of both Congress and the legislatures of the states involved is required.

The intention here is to prevent anyone from trying to create new states in an attempt to gain more electoral votes (that is, political power), as President Abraham Lincoln did with the illegal creation of West Virginia on June 20, 1863, when he violated the same clause in the US Constitution (Article 4, Section 3, Clause 1).[16]

---

16. Virginia never authorized the people in her western region to secede and form a new state. Thus, to this day "West Virginia" is not a legally formed state. Lincoln's encouragement and aid in this process was a clear infraction of the US Constitution.

ARTICLE 4, SECTION 3, CLAUSE 2

The Congress shall have power to dispose of and make all needful rules and regulations concerning the property of the Confederate States, including the lands thereof.

EXPLANATION: This clause gives the CS Congress collective authority over the land on which the CSA sits. In this way a uniform set of rules, established by elected officials, is imposed on the public property throughout all of the Confederate states.

Tacitly, this clause also give the CS government the power to create national parks, regulate wilderness areas, and in any way improve public land that is to be used by the Confederate people.

ARTICLE 4, SECTION 3, CLAUSE 3

The Confederate States may acquire new territory; and Congress shall have power to legislate and provide governments for the inhabitants of all territory belonging to the Confederate States, lying without the limits of the several States; and may permit them, at such times, and in such manner as it may by law provide, to form States to be admitted into the Confederacy. In all such territory the institution of negro slavery, as it now exists in the Confederate States, shall be recognized and protected by Congress and by the Territorial government; and the inhabitants of the several Confederate States and Territories shall have the right to take to such Territory any slaves lawfully held by them in any of the States or Territories of the Confederate States.

EXPLANATION: This clause stipulates that the CSA is endowed with the authority to expand geographically, and that any new states that are formed are to be governed by the CS Congress. Confederate-owned territories that have not yet been made into proper states may be formed into such according to CS law. Local government is to be divided into two tiers: one for the unformed territories and one for the states.

In addition, since the many problems associated with emancipation have not yet been resolved, the legality of slavery (or servitude, as it is more properly called) is "recognized and protected" by the CS Congress. As such, Confederate slave owners have the right to transport lawfully owned servants back and forth between into Confederate states and the Confederate territories.

ARTICLE 4, SECTION 3, CLAUSE 4

The Confederate States shall guarantee to every State that now is, or hereafter may become, a member of this Confederacy, a republican form of government; and shall protect each of them against invasion; and on application of the Legislature, (or of the Executive when the Legislature is not in session,) against domestic violence.

EXPLANATION: This clause lays out the sole *three* powers and responsibilities given to the CS government by the people:

1) All of the Confederate states, as well as territories that may eventually become Confederate states, are promised a republican form of government (that is, a small limited central government overseen by independent self-governing states, whose voting citizens are invested with the supreme power of the land, and whose laws are defined by the people and limited by a formal constitution).

2) The CS government promises to protect the Confederate states from foreign invasion.

3) The CS government promises to protect the Confederate states against homegrown violence (such as riots and terrorism originating from within the Confederacy). But the central government is prohibited from deploying armed federal forces into the states to aid in such cases, unless a state requests government assistance.

Beyond these three responsibilities, the CS government, like the original US government, has no other authorized powers. The purpose of these sharply limited powers is meant to prevent the growth of an out-of-control, overly powerful central government and the establishment of either a government dictatorship or state-run dictatorships.

Article 5

Constitutional Amendments

ARTICLE 5, SECTION 1, CLAUSE 1

Upon the demand of any three States, legally assembled in their several conventions, the Congress shall summon a convention of all the States, to take into consideration such amendments to the Constitution as the said States shall concur in suggesting at the time when the said demand is made; and should any of the proposed amendments to the Constitution be agreed on by the said convention, voting by States, and the same be ratified by the Legislatures of two-thirds of the several States, or by conventions in two-thirds thereof, as the one or the other mode of ratification may be proposed by the general convention, they shall thenceforward form a part of this Constitution. But no State shall, without its consent, be deprived of its equal representation in the Senate.

EXPLANATION: Article 5 establishes the process of making changes or adding revisions to the CS Constitution.

The only clause in Article 5, Clause 1 stipulates that amendments may be added to the CS Constitution by the following process:

1) Proposal: At least three Confederate states must call for a constitutional convention to discuss the proposed amendment(s).

2) Ratification: If two-thirds of the Confederate states approve (either through their legislatures or through conventions), the proposed amendment is ratified, becoming law.

3) A Confederate state cannot be denied equal representation (that is, the physical presence of its two senators) in the Senate.

Unlike the USA, where it is Congress who considers proposed amendments, in the CSA this job is given to the state legislatures. In both the CSA and the USA, however, it is the states who decide whether to ratify an amendment or not.

The process of amendment making was intentionally meant to be somewhat complex and difficult in order to prevent the addition of unnecessary, superficial, or harmful amendments. However, the idea of allowing occasional alterations to the CS Constitution is an important one: it insures that the document will adapt to a changing society while retaining the vital core precepts that were wisely built into it by the CS Founding Fathers (and before them, the US Founding Fathers).

Article 6

Government & Supreme Law

ARTICLE 6, CLAUSE 1

The Government established by this Constitution is the successor of the Provisional Government of the Confederate States of America, and all the laws passed by the latter shall continue in force until the same shall be repealed or modified; and all the officers appointed by the same shall remain in office until their successors are appointed and qualified, or the offices abolished.

EXPLANATION: With Article 6 the CS Constitution establishes a number of important legal provisions not covered elsewhere in the document.

Clause 1 begins by declaring that the now permanent CS government is a legal and binding continuation of the provisional (temporary) CS government, which had been set up earlier to carry the new country through its first seven state secessions.

Additionally, all laws made during the provisional government are to be carried forward into the permanent government, until they are either legally overturned or altered. All governmental officials appointed during the provisional government are to be retained as well.

ARTICLE 6, CLAUSE 2

All debts contracted and engagements entered into
before the adoption of this Constitution shall be as valid
against the Confederate States under this Constitution,
as under the Provisional Government.

EXPLANATION: In this clause the CS government promises to pay off
any debts it has incurred to the US government before it became a
constitutionally formed independent country: the CSA.

ARTICLE 6, CLAUSE 3

This Constitution, and the laws of the Confederate States made in pursuance thereof, and all treaties made, or which shall be made, under the authority of the Confederate States, shall be the supreme law of the land; and the judges in every State shall be bound thereby, anything in the constitution or laws of any State to the contrary notwithstanding.

EXPLANATION: In order to prevent possible future undermining of the CS Constitution by the Confederate states, this simple and direct clause declares that the Constitution is the "supreme law of the land," that judges (in whatever state they reside) are bound to abide by it, and that it has supremacy over any and all state laws.

ARTICLE 6, CLAUSE 4

The Senators and Representatives before mentioned, and the members of the several State Legislatures, and all executive and judicial officers, both of the Confederate States and of the several States, shall be bound by oath or affirmation to support this Constitution; but no religious test shall ever be required as a qualification to any office or public trust under the Confederate States.

EXPLANATION: This clause requires that all Confederate federal and state officials promise to uphold the CS Constitution. Additionally, because of the Constitution's separation of church and state (see Article 1, Section 9, Clause 12), an individual cannot be prevented from holding office due to his religion.

ARTICLE 6, CLAUSE 5

The enumeration, in the Constitution, of certain rights shall not be construed to deny or disparage others retained by the people of the several States.

EXPLANATION: This clause, the Ninth Amendment (of the Bill of Rights) to the US Constitution, prevents the central government from assuming powers, authority, and responsibilities not granted to it by the people of the Confederate states, in whom all sovereign power is vested.

The basic rights of the people are purposefully not spelled out here because they are listed elsewhere in the CS Constitution (see Article 1, Section 9, Clauses 12 through 19).

Either way, this all-embracing provision means that the central government is prohibited from interfering with or restricting the Confederate citizen's basic human, civil, social, religious, moral, ethical, and political rights and freedoms—for it was never given this power.

To the contrary, as clearly spelled out in Article 4, Section 3, Clause 4 of the CS Constitution, the CS central (federal) government possesses only three powers.

ARTICLE 6, CLAUSE 6

The powers not delegated to the Confederate States by the Constitution, nor prohibited by it to the States, are reserved to the States, respectively, or to the people thereof.

EXPLANATION: This clause, the all-important Tenth Amendment (of the Bill of Rights) to the US Constitution, asserts that the CS government is only permitted those few powers and responsibilities assigned to it by the people of the Confederate States of America (see Article 4, Section 3, Clause 4). It cannot step outside this provision, for all other powers belong to the people themselves.

Article 7

Ratification of the Constitution

ARTICLE 7, CLAUSE 1

The ratification of the conventions of five States shall be sufficient for the establishment of this Constitution between the States so ratifying the same.

EXPLANATION: This clause declares that it only takes the approval of five Confederate states to confirm the CS Constitution as official law.

ARTICLE 7, CLAUSE 2

When five States shall have ratified this Constitution, in the manner before specified, the Congress under the Provisional Constitution shall prescribe the time for holding the election of President and Vice President; and for the meeting of the Electoral College; and for counting the votes, and inaugurating the President. They shall, also, prescribe the time for holding the first election of members of Congress under this Constitution, and the time for assembling the same. Until the assembling of such Congress, the Congress under the Provisional Constitution shall continue to exercise the legislative powers granted them; not extending beyond the time limited by the Constitution of the Provisional Government.

Adopted unanimously by the Congress of the Confederate States of South Carolina, Georgia, Florida, Alabama, Mississippi, Louisiana, and Texas, sitting in convention at the capitol, the city of Montgomery, Ala., on the eleventh day of March, in the year eighteen hundred and Sixty-one.

SIGNATORIES

Howell Cobb, President of the Congress.

South Carolina: R. Barnwell Rhett, C. G. Memminger, Wm. Porcher Miles, James Chesnut, Jr., R. W. Barnwell, William W. Boyce, Lawrence M. Keitt, T. J. Withers.

Georgia: Francis S. Bartow, Martin J. Crawford, Benjamin H. Hill, Thos. R. R. Cobb.

Florida: Jackson Morton, J. Patton Anderson, Jas. B.

Owens.

Alabama: Richard W. Walker, Robt. H. Smith, Colin J. McRae, William P. Chilton, Stephen F. Hale, David P. Lewis, Tho. Fearn, Jno. Gill Shorter, J. L. M. Curry.

Mississippi: Alex. M. Clayton, James T. Harrison, William S. Barry, W. S. Wilson, Walker Brooke, W. P. Harris, J. A. P. Campbell.

Louisiana: Alex. de Clouet, C. M. Conrad, Duncan F. Kenner, Henry Marshall.

Texas: John Hemphill, Thomas N. Waul, John H. Reagan, Williamson S. Oldham, Louis T. Wigfall, John Gregg, William Beck Ochiltree.

EXPLANATION: This, the final clause of the CS Constitution, declares that after the document is signed into law by the ratification of five Confederate states, the CS Congress will set a date for the election of the CS president and the CS vice president; for a gathering of the Electoral College; for tallying the votes; and for swearing in the president. Congress will also set up a date for the first election of the members of its own body, according to the rules of the Constitution.

Finally, this clause stipulates that until all of this occurs, the present Congress will continue to operate under the laws of the temporary Constitution (made obsolete by this document).

The CS Constitution is then approved by the seven states that are currently members of the CSA: South Carolina, Georgia, Florida, Alabama, Mississippi, Louisiana, and Texas (four more Southern states, Virginia, Arkansas, Tennessee, North Carolina, and portions of Kentucky and Missouri, would join the CSA shortly thereafter). Howell Cobb, president of the CS Congress, along with representatives from these seven states, sign their names to last page of the Constitution.

Location: the temporary Confederate Capitol at Montgomery, Alabama. Date: March 11, 1861.

President of the Montgomery Convention and the provisional Confederate Congress, Howell Cobb.

SUGGESTED READING

AUTHOR'S NOTE: MANY OF THE FOLLOWING BOOKS ARE ANTI-SOUTH (SOME IN THE EXTREME) AND ARE THEREFORE OF LITTLE VALUE HISTORICALLY. HOWEVER, THE STUDY OF BIASED PROPAGANDA CAN BE JUST AS IMPORTANT AS FACTUAL MATERIAL.

Adams, Charles. *When in the Course of Human Events: Arguing the Case for Southern Secession.* Lanham, MD: Rowman and Littlefield, 2000.

Adams, Henry (ed.). *Documents Relating to New-England Federalism, 1800-1815.* Boston, MA: Little, Brown, and Co., 1877.

Andrews, Elisha Benjamin. *The United States in Our Own Time: A History From Reconstruction to Expansion.* 1895. New York, NY: Charles Scribner's Sons, 1903 ed.

Anonymous. *Life of John C. Calhoun: Presenting a Condensed History of Political Events, From 1811 to 1843.* New York, NY: Harper and Brothers, 1843.

Ashe, Captain Samuel A'Court. *A Southern View of the Invasion of the Southern States and War of 1861-1865.* 1935. Crawfordville, GA: Ruffin Flag Co., 1938 ed.

Ashworth, John. *Slavery, Capitalism, and Politics in the Antebellum Republic.* 2 vols. New York, NY: Cambridge University Press, 2007.

Baepler, Paul (ed.). *White Slaves, African Masters: An Anthology of American Barbary Captivity Narratives.* Chicago, IL: University of Chicago Press, 1999.

Bailey, Anne C. *African Voices of the Atlantic Slave Trade: Beyond the Silence and the Shame.* Boston, MA: Beacon Press, 2005.

Bailyn, Bernard, Robert Dallek, David Brion Davis, David Herbert Donald, John L. Thomas, and Gordon S. Wood. *The Great Republic: A History of the American People.* 1977. Lexington, MA: D. C. Heath and Co., 1992 ed.

Baker, George E. (ed.). *The Works of William H. Seward.* 5 vols. 1861. Boston, MA: Houghton, Mifflin and Co., 1888 ed.

Bancroft, Frederic, and William A. Dunning (eds.). *The Reminiscences of Carl Schurz.* 3 vols. New York, NY: McClure Co., 1909.

Barrow, Charles Kelly, J. H. Segars, and R. B. Rosenburg (eds.). *Black Confederates.* 1995. Gretna, LA: Pelican Publishing Co., 2001 ed.

——. *Forgotten Confederates: An Anthology About Black Southerners.* Saint Petersburg, FL: Southern Heritage Press, 1997.

Bartlett, Irving H. *John C. Calhoun: A Biography.* New York, NY: W. W. Norton, 1994.

Bateman, William O. *Political and Constitutional Law of the United States of America.* St. Louis, MO: G. I. Jones and Co., 1876.

Baxter, Maurice G. *Henry Clay and the American System.* Lexington, KY: University Press of Kentucky, 2004.

Beard, Charles A., and Birl E. Schultz. *Documents on the State-Wide Initiative, Referendum and Recall.* New York, NY: Macmillan, 1912.

Beard, Charles A., and Mary R. Beard. *The Rise of American Civilization.* 1927. New York, NY: MacMillan, 1930 ed.

Beck, Glenn. *Glenn Beck's Common Sense: The Case Against an Out-of-Control Government, Inspired by Thomas Paine*. New York, NY: Threshold, 2009.

Belz, Herman. *Abraham Lincoln, Constitutionalism, and Equal Rights in the Civil War Era*. Bronx, NY: Fordham University Press, 1997.

Bennett, Lerone. *Forced into Glory: Abraham Lincoln's White Dream*. Chicago, IL: Johnson Publishing Co., 2000.

Benton, Thomas Hart. *Thirty Years View; or A History of the Working of the American Government for Thirty Years, From 1820 to 1850*. 2 vols. New York, NY: D. Appleton and Co., 1854.

Bergh, Albert Ellery (ed.). *The Writings of Thomas Jefferson*. 20 vols. Washington, D.C.: Thomas Jefferson Memorial Association of the U.S., 1905.

Bernhard, Winfred E. A. (ed.). *Political Parties in American History* (Vol. 1, 1789-1828). New York, NY: G. P. Putnams' Sons, 1973.

Berwanger, Eugene H. *The Frontier Against Slavery: Western Anti-Negro Prejudice and the Slavery Extension Controversy*. 1967. Urbana, IL: University of Illinois Press, 1971 ed.

Beschloss, Michael R. *Presidential Courage: Brave Leaders and How They Changed America, 1789-1989*. New York, NY: Simon and Schuster, 2007.

Bledsoe, Albert Taylor. *A Theodicy; or a Vindication of the Divine Glory, as Manifested in the Constitution and Government of the Moral World*. New York, NY: Carlton and Porter, 1856.

Bliss, William Dwight Porter (ed.). *The Encyclopedia of Social Reform*. New York, NY: Funk and Wagnalls, 1897.

Bowen, Catherine Drinker. *John Adams and the American Revolution*. 1949. New York, NY: Grosset and Dunlap, 1977 ed.

Bradford, James C. (ed.). *Atlas of American Military History*. New York, NY: Oxford University Press, 2003.

Brady, James S. (ed.). *Ronald Reagan: A Man True to His Word - A Portrait of the 40th President of the United States In His Own Words*. Washington D.C.: National Federation of Republican Women, 1984.

Brinkley, Alan. *The Unfinished Nation: A Concise History of the American People*. 1993. Boston, MA: McGraw-Hill, 2000 ed.

Buchanan, James. *The Works of James Buchanan*. 12 vols. Philadelphia, PA: J. B. Lippincott Co., 1911.

Buchanan, Patrick J. *A Republic, Not an Empire: Reclaiming America's Destiny*. Washington, D.C.: Regenry, 1999.

Buckingham, James Silk. *The Slave States of America*. 2 vols. London, UK: Fisher, Son, and Co., 1842.

Burns, James MacGregor, and Jack Walter Peltason. *Government by the People: The Dynamics of American National, State, and Local Government*. 1952. Englewood Cliffs, NJ: Prentice-Hall, 1964 ed.

Burns, James MacGregor, Jack Walter Peltason, Thomas E. Cronin, David B. Magleby, and David M. O'Brien. *Government by the People* (National Version). 1952. Upper Saddle River, NJ: Prentice Hall, 2001-2002 ed.

Calvert, Thomas H. *The Federal Statutes Annotated*. 10 vols. Northport, NY: Edward Thompson, 1905.

Cannon, Devereaux D., Jr. *The Flags of the Confederacy: An Illustrated History*. Memphis, TN: St. Luke's Press, 1988.

Chadwick, Bruce. *The Two American Presidents: A Dual Biography of Abraham Lincoln and Jefferson Davis*. New York, NY: Citadel, 1999.

Chesnut, Mary. *A Diary From Dixie: As Written by Mary Boykin Chesnut, Wife of James Chesnut, Jr., United States Senator from South Carolina, 1859-1861, and afterward an Aide to Jefferson Davis and a Brigadier-General in the Confederate Army*. (Isabella D. Martin and Myrta Lockett Avary, eds.). New York, NY: D. Appleton and Co., 1905 ed.

Civil War Society, The. *Civil War Battles: An Illustrated Encyclopedia*. 1997. New York, NY: Gramercy, 1999 ed.

——. *The Civil War Society's Encyclopedia of the Civil War*. New York, NY: Wings Books, 1997.

Collier, Christopher, and James Lincoln Collier. *Decision in Philadelphia: The Constitutional Convention of 1787*. 1986. New York, NY: Ballantine, 1987 ed.

Conner, Frank. *The South Under Siege, 1830-2000: A History of the Relations Between the North and the South*. Newnan, GA: Collards Publishing Co., 2002.

Cooper, William J., Jr. *Jefferson Davis, American*. New York, NY: Vintage, 2000.

——. (ed.). *Jefferson Davis: The Essential Writings*. New York, NY: Random House, 2003.

Crallé, Richard Kenner. (ed.). *The Works of John C. Calhoun*. 6 vols. New York: NY: D. Appleton and Co., 1853-1888.

Craven, John J. *Prison Life of Jefferson Davis*. New York: NY: Carelton, 1866.

Crawford, Samuel Wylie. *The Genesis of the Civil War: The Story of Sumter, 1860-1861*. New York, NY: Charles L. Webster and Co., 1887.

Crocker, H. W., III. *The Politically Incorrect Guide to the Civil War*. Washington, D.C.: Regnery, 2008.

Cross, Harold A. *They Sleep Beneath the Mockingbird: Mississippi Burial Sites and Biographies of Confederate Generals*. Saint Petersburg, FL: Southern Heritage Press, 1997.

Dabney, Robert Lewis. *A Defense of Virginia and the South*. Dahlonega, GA: Confederate Reprint Co., 1999.

Daniel, John M. *The Richmond Examiner During the War*. New York, NY: John M. Daniel, 1868.

Daniel, John W. *Life and Reminiscences of Jefferson Davis by Distinguished Men of His Time*. Baltimore, MD: R. H. Woodward, and Co., 1890.

Davis, Jefferson. *The Rise and Fall of the Confederate Government*. 2 vols. New York, NY: D. Appleton and Co., 1881.

——. *A Short History of the Confederate States of America*. New York, NY: Belford, 1890.

Davis, Varina. *Jefferson Davis: Ex-President of the Confederate States of America - A Memoir by His Wife*. 2 vols. New York, NY: Belford Co., 1890.

Davis, William C. *Jefferson Davis: The Man and His Hour*. New York, NY: HarperCollins, 1991.

——. *An Honorable Defeat: The Last Days of the Confederate Government*. New York, NY: Harcourt, 2001.

——. *Look Away: A History of the Confederate States of America*. 2002. New York, NY: Free Press, 2003 ed.

Dawson, Sarah Morgan. *A Confederate Girl's Diary*. London, UK: William Heinemann, 1913.

DeGregorio, William A. *The Complete Book of U.S. Presidents*. 1984. New York, NY: Barricade, 1993 ed.

Denson, John V. (ed.). *Reassessing the Presidency: The Rise of the Executive State and the Decline of Freedom*. Auburn, AL: Mises Institute, 2001.

Derosa, Marshall L. *The Confederate Constitution of 1861: An Inquiry into American Constitutionalism*. Columbia, MO: University of Missouri Press, 1991.

Derry, Joseph T. *Story of the Confederate States, or, History of the War for Southern Independence*. Richmond, VA: B. F. Johnson, 1898.

Desty, Robert. *The Constitution of the United States*. San Francisco, CA: Sumner Whitney and Co., 1881.

Dicey, Edward. *Six Months in the Federal States*. 2 vols. London, UK: Macmillan and Co., 1863.

DiLorenzo, Thomas J. "The Great Centralizer: Abraham Lincoln and the War Between the States." *The Independent Review*, Vol. 3, No. 2, Fall 1998, pp. 243-271.

——. *The Real Lincoln: A New Look at Abraham Lincoln, His Agenda, and an Unnecessary War*. Three Rivers, MI: Three Rivers Press, 2003.

——. *Lincoln Unmasked: What You're Not Supposed to Know About Dishonest Abe*. New York, NY: Crown Forum, 2006.

——. *Hamilton's Curse: How Jefferson's Archenemy Betrayed the American Revolution—and What It Means for America Today*. New York, NY: Crown Forum, 2008.

DiLorenzo, Thomas J., and Joseph A. Morris. *Abraham Lincoln: Friend or Foe of Freedom?* Chicago, IL: Heartland Institute, 2008.

Douglass, Frederick. *Narrative of the Life of Frederick Douglass: An American Slave*. 1845. New York, NY: Signet, 1997 ed.

——. *The Life and Times of Frederick Douglass, From 1817 to 1882*. London, UK: Christian Age Office, 1882.

Dunbar, Rowland (ed.). *Jefferson Davis, Constitutionalist: His Letters, Papers, and Speeches*. 10 vols. Jackson, MS: Mississippi Department of Archives and History, 1923.

Durden, Robert F. *The Gray and the Black: The Confederate Debate on Emancipation*. Baton Rouge, LA: Louisiana State University Press, 1972.

Early, Jubal A. *A Memoir of the Last Year of the War for Independence in the Confederate States of America*. Lynchburg, VA: Charles W. Button, 1867.

Eaton, Clement. *A History of the Southern Confederacy*. 1945. New York, NY: Free Press, 1966 ed.

——. *Jefferson Davis*. New York, NY: Free Press, 1977.

Edmonds, Franklin Spencer. *Ulysses S. Grant*. Philadelphia, PA: George W. Jacobs and Co., 1915.

Egerton, Douglas R. *Year of Meteors: Stephen Douglas, Abraham Lincoln, and the Election that Brought on the Civil War*. New York, NY: Bloomsbury Press, 2010.

Elliot, Jonathan. *The Debates in the Several State Conventions on the Adoption of the Federal Constitution, As Recommended by the General Convention at Philadelphia in 1787*. 5 vols. Philadelphia, PA: J. B. Lippincott, 1891.

Emerson, Bettie Alder Calhoun. *Historic Southern Monuments: Representative Memorials of the Heroic Dead of the Southern Confederacy*. New York, NY: Neale Publishing Co., 1911.

Encyclopedia Britannica: A New Survey of Universal Knowledge. 1768. Chicago, IL/London, UK: Encyclopedia Britannica, 1955 ed.

Evans, Clement Anselm (ed.). *Confederate Military History: A Library of Confederate States History, in Twelve Volumes, Written By Distinguished Men of the South*. 12 vols. Atlanta, GA: Confederate Publishing Co., 1899.

Evans, Lawrence B. (ed.). *Writings of George Washington*. New York, NY: G. P. Putnam's Sons, 1908.

Farrow, Anne, Joel Lang, and Jennifer Frank. *Complicity: How the North Promoted, Prolonged, and Profited From Slavery*. New York, NY: Ballantine, 2005.

Fehrenbacher, Don E. *The Slaveholding Republic: An Account of the United States Government's Relations to Slavery*. New York, NY: Oxford University Press, 2002.

Finkelman, Paul. *Dred Scott v. Sanford: A Brief History With Documents*. Boston, MA: Bedford Books, 1997.

Fite, Emerson David. *Social and Industrial Conditions in the North During the Civil War*. New York, NY: Macmillan, 1910.

——. *The Presidential Election of 1860*. New York, NY: MacMillan, 1911.

House Documents, 64th Congress, 1st Session, December 6, 1915, to September 8, 1916, Vol. 145. Washington, D.C.: Government Printing Office, 1916.

Fogel, Robert William, and Stanley L. Engerman. *Time On the Cross: The Economics of American Negro Slavery*. Boston, MA: Little, Brown, and Co., 1974.

Foley, John P. (ed.). *The Jeffersonian Cyclopedia*. New York, NY: Funk and Wagnalls, 1900.

Foner, Eric. *Free Soil, Free Labor, Free Men: The Ideology of the Republican Party Before the Civil War*. New York, NY: Oxford University Press, 1970.

——. *Reconstruction: America's Unfinished Revolution, 1863-1877*. 1988. New York, NY: Harper and Row, 1989 ed.

Foote, Shelby. *The Civil War: A Narrative, Fort Sumter to Perryville, Vol. 1*. 1958. New York, NY: Vintage, 1986 ed.

——. *The Civil War: A Narrative, Fredericksburg to Meridian, Vol. 2*. 1963. New York, NY: Vintage, 1986 ed.

——. *The Civil War: A Narrative, Red River to Appomattox, Vol. 3*. 1974. New York, NY: Vintage, 1986 ed.

Ford, Paul Leicester (ed.). *The Works of Thomas Jefferson*. 12 vols. New York, NY: G. P. Putnam's Sons, 1904.

Ford, Worthington Chauncey (ed.). *A Cycle of Adams Letters*. 2 vols. Boston, MA: Houghton Mifflin, 1920.

Forman, S. E. *The Life and Writings of Thomas Jefferson*. Indianapolis, IN: Bowen-Merrill, 1900.

Fowler, John D. *The Confederate Experience Reader: Selected Documents and Essays*. New York, NY: Routledge, 2007.

Fowler, William Chauncey. *The Sectional Controversy; or Passages in the Political History of the United States, Including the Causes of the War Between the Sections*. New York, NY: Charles Scribner, 1864.

Fox, Gustavus Vasa. *Confidential Correspondence of Gustavus Vasa Fox, Assistant Secretary of the Navy, 1861-1865*. 2 vols. 1918. New York, NY: Naval History Society, 1920 ed.

Franklin, Benjamin. *The Complete Works of Benjamin Franklin*. 10 vols. New York, NY: G. P. Putnam's Sons, 1887.

Franklin, John Hope. *Reconstruction After the Civil War*. Chicago, IL: University of Chicago Press, 1961.

Furnas, J. C. *The Americans: A Social History of the United States, 1587-1914*. New York, NY: G. P. Putnam's Sons, 1969.

Galenson, David W. *White Servitude in Colonial America*. New York, NY: Cambridge University Press, 1981.

Garraty, John A., and Robert A. McCaughey. *A Short History of the American Nation*. 1966. New York, NY: HarperCollins, 1989 ed.

Gordon, Armistead Churchill. *Figures From American History: Jefferson Davis*. New York, NY: Charles Scribner's Sons, 1918.

Graham, John Remington. *A Constitutional History of Secession*. Gretna, LA: Pelican Publishing Co., 2003.

——. *Blood Money: The Civil War and the Federal Reserve*. Gretna, LA: Pelican Publishing Co., 2006.

Greenhow, Rose O'Neal. *My Imprisonment and the First Year of Abolition Rule at Washington*. London, UK: Richard Bentley, 1863.

Grimsley, Mark. *The Hard Hand of War: Union Military Policy Toward Southern Civilians, 1861-1865*. 1995. Cambridge, UK: Cambridge University Press, 1997 ed.

Grissom, Michael Andrew. *Southern By the Grace of God*. 1988. Gretna, LA: Pelican Publishing Co., 1995 ed.

Hacker, Louis Morton. *The Shaping of the American Tradition*. New York, NY: Columbia University Press, 1947.

Hall, B. C., and C. T. Wood. *The South: A Two-step Odyssey on the Backroads of the Enchanted Land*. New York, NY: Touchstone, 1996.

Hall, Kermit L. (ed). *The Oxford Companion to the Supreme Court of the United States*. New York, NY: Oxford University Press, 1992.

Hamblin, Ken. *Pick a Better Country: An Unassuming Colored Guy Speaks His Mind About America*. New York, NY: Touchstone, 1997.

Hamilton, Neil A. *Rebels and Renegades: A Chronology of Social and Political Dissent in the United States*. New York, NY: Routledge, 2002.

Hannity, Sean. *Let Freedom Ring: Winning the War of Liberty Over Liberalism*. New York, NY: HarperCollins, 2002.

Hansen, Harry. *The Civil War: A History*. 1961. Harmondsworth, UK: Mentor, 1991 ed.

Harding, Samuel Bannister. *The Contest Over the Ratification of the Federal Constitution in the State of*

Massachusetts. New York, NY: Longmans, Green, and Co., 1896.

Harrell, David Edwin, Jr., Edwin S. Gaustad, John B. Boles, Sally Foreman Griffith, Randall M. Miller, and Randall B. Woods. *Unto a Good Land: A History of the American People*. Grand Rapids, MI: William B. Eerdmans, 2005.

Hartzell, Josiah. *The Genesis of the Republican Party*. Canton, OH: n.p., 1890.

Harwell, Richard B. (ed.). *The Confederate Reader: How the South Saw the War*. 1957. Mineola, NY: Dover, 1989 ed.

Hattaway, Herman, and Archer Jones. *How the North Won: A Military History of the Civil War*. 1983. Champaign, IL: University of Illinois Press, 1991 ed.

Hawthorne, Julian (ed.). *Orations of American Orators*. 2 vols. New York, NY: Colonial Press, 1900.

Hawthorne, Julian, James Schouler, and Elisha Benjamin Andrews. *United States, From the Discovery of the North American Continent Up to the Present Time*. 9 vols. New York, NY: Co-operative Publication Society, 1894.

Heidler, David S., and Jeanne T. Heidler. *Henry Clay: The Essential American*. New York, NY: Random House, 2010.

Helper, Hinton Rowan. *The Impending Crisis of the South: How to Meet It*. New York, NY: A. B. Burdick, 1860.

Henry, Robert Selph (ed.). *The Story of the Confederacy*. 1931. New York, NY: Konecky and Konecky, 1999 ed.

Hervey, Anthony. *Why I Wave the Confederate Flag, Written By a Black Man: The End of Niggerism and the Welfare State*. Oxford, UK: Trafford Publishing, 2006.

Hesseltine, William B. *Lincoln and the War Governors*. New York, NY: Alfred A. Knopf, 1948.

Hickey, William. *The Constitution of the United States*. Philadelphia, PA: T. K. and P. G. Collins, 1853.

Hinkle, Don. *Embattled Banner: A Reasonable Defense of the Confederate Battle Flag*. Paducah, KY: Turner Publishing Co., 1997.

Hoffman, Michael A., II. *They Were White and They Were Slaves: The Untold History of the Enslavement of Whites in Early America*. Dresden, NY: Wiswell Ruffin House, 1993.

Hofstadter, Richard. *The American Political Tradition, and the Men Who Made It*. New York, NY: Alfred A. Knopf, 1948.

Holland, Jesse J. *Black Men Built the Capitol: Discovering African-American History in and Around Washington, D.C.* Guilford, CT: The Globe Pequot Press, 2007.

Howe, Daniel Wait. *Political History of Secession*. New York, NY: G. P. Putnam's Sons, 1914.

Howe, Henry. *Historical Collections of Virginia*. Charleston, SC: William R. Babcock, 1852.

Ingersoll, Thomas G., and Robert E. O'Connor. *Politics and Structure: Essential of American National Government*. North Scituate, MA: Duxbury Press, 1979.

Jefferson, Thomas. *Notes on the State of Virginia*. Boston, MA: H. Sprague, 1802.

Jenkins, John S. *The Life of James Knox Polk, Late President of the United States*. Auburn, NY: James M. Alden, 1850.

Jensen, Merrill. *The New Nation: A History of the United States During the Confederation, 1781-1789*. New York, NY: Vintage, 1950.

——. *The Articles of Confederation: An Interpretation of the Social-Constitutional History of the American Revolution, 1774-1781*. Madison, WI: University of Wisconsin Press, 1959.

Johnson, Benjamin Heber. *Making of the American West: People and Perspectives*. Santa Barbara, CA: ABC-Clio, 2007.

Johnson, Clint. *The Politically Incorrect Guide to the South (and Why It Will Rise Again)*. Washington, D.C.: Regnery, 2006.

Johnson, Ludwell H. *North Against South: The American Iliad, 1848-1877*. 1978. Columbia, SC: Foundation for American Education, 1993 ed.

Johnson, Michael, and James L. Roark. *Black Masters: A Free Family of Color in the Old South*. New York, NY: W.W. Norton, 1984.

Johnson, Robert Underwood (ed.). *Battles and Leaders of the Civil War*. 4 vols. New York, NY: The Century Co., 1884-1888.

Jones, John Beauchamp. *A Rebel War Clerk's Diary at the Confederate States Capital*. 2 vols. in 1. Philadelphia, PA: J. B. Lippincott and Co., 1866.

Julian, George Washington. *Speeches on Political Questions*. New York, NY: Hurd and Houghton, 1872.

Kane, Joseph Nathan. *Facts About the Presidents: A Compilation of Biographical and Historical Data*. 1959. New York, NY: Ace, 1976 ed.

Kelly, Alfred H., Winfred A. Harbison, and Herman Belz. *The American Constitution: Its Origins and Development* (Vol. 2). 1965. New York, NY: W.W. Norton, 1991 ed.

Kennedy, James Ronald, and Walter Donald Kennedy. *Why Not Freedom!: America's Revolt Against Big Government*. Gretna, LA: Pelican Publishing Co., 2005.

Kettell, Thomas Prentice. *History of the Great Rebellion*. Hartford, CT: L. Stebbins, 1865.

Kinder, Hermann, and Werner Hilgemann. *The Anchor Atlas of World History: From the French Revolution to the American Bicentennial*. 2 vols. Garden City, NY: Anchor, 1978.

King, Charles R. (ed.). *The Life and Correspondence of Rufus King*. 6 vols. New York, NY: G. P. Putnam's Sons, 1897.

Lee, Charles Robert, Jr. *The Confederate Constitutions*. Chapel Hill, NC: University of North Carolina Press, 1963.

Lemire, Elise. *Black Walden: Slavery and Its Aftermath in Concord, Massachusetts*. Philadelphia, PA: University of Pennsylvania Press, 2009.

Lester, Charles Edwards. *Life and Public Services of Charles Sumner*. New York, NY: U.S. Publishing Co., 1874.

Lewis, Lloyd. *Myths After Lincoln*. 1929. New York, NY: The Press of the Reader's Club, 1941 ed.

LeVert, Suzanne (ed.). *The Civil War Society's Encyclopedia of the Civil War*. New York, NY: Wings Books, 1997.

Levin, Mark R. *Liberty and Tyranny: A Conservative Manifesto*. New York, NY: Threshold, 2009.

Litwack, Leon F. *North of Slavery: The Negro in the Free States, 1790-1860*. Chicago, IL: University of Chicago Press, 1961.

———. *Been in the Storm So Long: The Aftermath of Slavery*. New York, NY: Vintage, 1980.

Livermore, Thomas L. *Numbers and Losses in the Civil War in America, 1861-65*. 1900. Carlisle, PA: John Kallmann, 1996 ed.

Livingstone, William. *Livingstone's History of the Republican Party*. 2 vols. Detroit, MI: William Livingstone, 1900.

Locke, John. *Two Treatises of Government* (Mark Goldie, ed.). 1924. London, UK: Everyman, 1998 ed.

Lodge, Henry Cabot (ed.). *The Works of Alexander Hamilton*. 12 vols. New York, NY: G. P. Putnam's Sons, 1904.

MacDonald, William. *Select Documents Illustrative of the History of the United States 1776-1861*. New York, NY: Macmillan, 1897.

Madison, James. *Letters and Other Writings of James Madison, Fourth President of the United States*. 4 vols. Philadelphia, PA: J. B. Lippincott and Co., 1865.

Main, Jackson Turner. *The Anti-Federalists: Critics of the Constitution, 1781-1788*. 1961. New York, NY: W. W. Norton and Co., 1974 ed.

Malone, Laurence J. *Opening the West: Federal Internal Improvements Before 1860*. Westport, CT: Greenwood Press, 1998.

Manegold, Catherine S. *The Forgotten History of Slavery in the North*. Princeton, NJ: Princeton University Press, 2010.

Mayer, David N. *The Constitutional Thought of Thomas Jefferson*. Charlottesville, VA: University of Virginia Press, 1995.

McCullough, David. *John Adams*. New York, NY: Touchstone, 2001.

McDonald, Forrest. *States' Rights and the Union: Imperium in Imperio, 1776-1876*. Lawrence, KS: University Press of Kansas, 2000.

McElroy, Robert. *Jefferson Davis: The Unreal and the Real*. 1937. New York, NY: Smithmark, 1995 ed.

McGehee, Jacob Owen. *Causes That Led to the War Between the States*. Atlanta, GA: A. B. Caldwell, 1915.

McGuire, Hunter, and George L. Christian. *The Confederate Cause and Conduct in the War Between the States*. Richmond, VA: L. H. Jenkins, 1907.

McMaster, John Bach. *Our House Divided: A History of the People of the United States During Lincoln's Administration*. 1927. New York, NY: Premier, 1961 ed.

McPherson, Edward. *The Political History of the United States of America, During the Great Rebellion (From November 6, 1860, to July 4, 1864)*. Washington, D.C.: Philp and Solomons, 1864.

——. *The Political History of the United States of America, During the Period of Reconstruction, (From April 15, 1865, to July 15, 1870,) Including a Classified Summary of the Legislation of the Thirty-ninth, Fortieth, and Forty-first Congresses*. Washington, D.C.: Solomons and Chapman, 1875.

Meltzer, Milton. *Slavery: A World History*. 2 vols. in 1. 1971. New York, NY: Da Capo Press, 1993 ed.

Meriwether, Elizabeth Avery. *Facts and Falsehoods Concerning the War on the South, 1861-1865*. (Originally written under the pseudonym "George Edmonds.") Memphis, TN: A. R. Taylor, 1904.

Miller, John Chester. *The Wolf By the Ears: Thomas Jefferson and Slavery*. 1977. Charlottesville, VA: University Press of Virginia, 1994 ed.

Miller, Marion Mills (ed.). *Great Debates in American History*. 14 vols. New York, NY: Current Literature, 1913.

Minor, Charles Landon Carter. *The Real Lincoln: From the Testimony of His Contemporaries*. Richmond, VA: Everett Waddey Co., 1904.

Moore, Frank (ed.). *The Rebellion Record: A Diary of American Events*. 12 vols. New York, NY: G. P. Putnam, 1861.

Moore, George Henry. *Notes on the History of Slavery in Massachusetts*. New York, NY: D. Appleton and Co., 1866.

Napolitano, Andrew P. *The Constitution in Exile: How the Federal Government has Seized Power by Rewriting the Supreme Law of the Land*. Nashville, TN: Nelson Current, 2006.

——. *A Nation of Sheep*. Nashville, TN: Thomas Nelson, 2007.

Neely, Mark E., Jr. *The Fate of Liberty: Abraham Lincoln and Civil Liberties*. New York, NY: Oxford University Press, 1991.

Nicolay, John G., and John Hay (eds.). *Abraham Lincoln: A History*. 10 vols. New York, NY: The Century Co., 1890.

——. *Complete Works of Abraham Lincoln*. 12 vols. 1894. New York, NY: Francis D. Tandy Co., 1905 ed.

——. *Abraham Lincoln: Complete Works*. 12 vols. 1894. New York, NY: The Century Co., 1907 ed.

Nivola, Pietro S., and David H. Rosenbloom (eds.). *Classic Readings in American Politics*. New York, NY: St. Martin's Press, 1986.

Norwood, Thomas Manson. *A True Vindication of the South*. Savannah, GA: Citizens and Southern Bank, 1917.

Oglesby, Thaddeus K. *Some Truths of History: A Vindication of the South Against the Encyclopedia Britannica and Other Maligners*. Atlanta, GA: Byrd Printing, 1903.

Olmsted, Frederick Law. *A Journey in the Seaboard Slave States, With Remarks on Their Economy*. New York, NY: Dix and Edwards, 1856.

ORA, full title: *The War of the Rebellion: A Compilation of the Official Records of the Union and Confederate Armies*. (Multiple volumes.) Washington, D.C.: Government Printing Office, 1880.

Owsley, Frank Lawrence. *King Cotton Diplomacy: Foreign Relations of the Confederate States of America*. 1931. Chicago, IL: University of Chicago Press, 1959 ed.

Parry, Melanie (ed.). *Chambers Biographical Dictionary*. 1897. Edinburgh, Scotland: Chambers Harrap, 1998 ed.

Patrick, Rembert W. *Jefferson Davis and His Cabinet*. Baton Rouge, LA: Louisiana State University Press, 1944.

Paul, Ron. *The Revolution: A Manifesto*. New York, NY: Grand Central Publishing, 2008.

Perkins, Henry C. *Northern Editorials on Secession*. 2 vols. D. Appleton and Co., 1942.

Peterson, Merrill D. (ed.). *James Madison, A Biography in His Own Words*. (First published posthumously in 1840.) New York, NY: Harper and Row, 1974 ed.

——. (ed.). *Thomas Jefferson: Writings, Autobiography, A Summary View of the Rights of British America, Notes on the State of Virginia, Public Papers, Addresses, Messages and Replies, Miscellany, Letters*. New York, NY: Literary Classics, 1984.

Phillips, Wendell. *Speeches, Letters, and Lectures*. Boston, MA: Lee and Shepard, 1894.

Piatt, Donn. *Memories of the Men Who Saved the Union*. New York, NY: Belford, Clarke, and Co., 1887.

Pollard, Edward A. *Southern History of the War*. 2 vols. in 1. New York, NY: Charles B. Richardson, 1866.

——. *The Lost Cause*. 1867. Chicago, IL: E. B. Treat, 1890 ed.

——. *The Lost Cause Regained*. New York, NY: G. W. Carlton and Co., 1868.

——. *Life of Jefferson Davis, With a Secret History of the Southern Confederacy, Gathered "Behind the Scenes in Richmond."* Philadelphia, PA: National Publishing Co., 1869.

Powell, Edward Payson. *Nullification and Secession in the United States: A History of the Six Attempts During the First Century of the Republic*. New York, NY: G. P. Putnam's Sons, 1897.

Rable, George C. *The Confederate Republic: A Revolution Against Politics*. Chapel Hill, NC: University of North Carolina Press, 1994.

Randall, James Garfield. *Lincoln: The Liberal Statesman*. New York, NY: Dodd, Mead and Co., 1947.

Randolph, Thomas Jefferson (ed.). *Memoir, Correspondence, and Miscellanies, from the Papers of Thomas Jefferson*. 4 vols. Charlottesville, VA: F. Carr and Co., 1829.

Rawle, William. *A View of the Constitution of the United States of America*. Philadelphia, PA: Philip H. Nicklin, 1829.

Rayner, B. L. *Sketches of the Life, Writings, and Opinions of Thomas Jefferson*. New York, NY: Alfred Francis and William Boardman, 1832.

Remsburg, John B. *Abraham Lincoln: Was He a Christian?* New York, NY: The Truth Seeker Co., 1893.

Reports of Committees of the Senate of the United States (for the Thirty-eighth Congress). Washington, D.C.: Government Printing Office, 1864.

Rhodes, James Ford. *History of the United States from the Compromise of 1850 to the Final Restoration of Home Rule at the South in 1877*. 7 vols. 1895. New York, NY: Macmillan Co., 1907 ed.

Richardson, James Daniel (ed.). *A Compilation of the Messages and Papers of the Confederacy*. 2 vols. Nashville, TN: United States Publishing Co., 1905.

Richardson, John Anderson. *Richardson's Defense of the South*. Atlanta, GA: A. B. Caldwell, 1914.

Rives, John (ed.). *Abridgement of the Debates of Congress: From 1789 to 1856* (Vol. 13). New York, NY: D. Appleton and Co., 1860.

Roberts, Paul M. *United States History: Review Text*. 1966. New York, NY: Amsco School Publications, 1970 ed.

Rosenbaum, Robert A., and Douglas Brinkley (eds.). *The Penguin Encyclopedia of American History*. New York, NY: Viking, 2003.

Rouse, Adelaide Louise (ed.). *National Documents: State Papers So Arranged as to Illustrate the Growth of Our Country From 1606 to the Present Day*. New York, NY: Unit Book Publishing Co.,

1906.

Rowland, Dunbar (ed.). *Jefferson Davis, Constitutionalist: His Letters, Papers, and Speeches*. 10 vols. Jackson, MS: Mississippi Department of Archives and History,1923.

Rozwenc, Edwin Charles (ed.). *The Causes of the American Civil War*. 1961. Lexington, MA: D. C. Heath and Co., 1972 ed.

Rutherford, Mildred Lewis. *Four Addresses*. Birmingham, AL: The Mildred Rutherford Historical Circle, 1916.

——. *A True Estimate of Abraham Lincoln and Vindication of the South*. N.p., n.d.

——. *Truths of History: A Historical Perspective of the Civil War From the Southern Viewpoint*. Confederate Reprint Co., 1920.

——. *The South Must Have Her Rightful Place In History*. N.p.: Athens, GA, 1923.

Rutland, Robert Allen. *The Birth of the Bill of Rights, 1776-1791*. 1955. Boston, MA: Northeastern University Press, 1991 ed.

Samuel, Bunford. *Secession and Constitutional Liberty*. 2 vols. New York, NY: Neale Publishing, 1920.

Sandburg, Carl. *Abraham Lincoln: The War Years*. 4 vols. New York, NY: Harcourt, Brace and World, 1939.

——. *Storm Over the Land: A Profile of the Civil War*. 1939. Old Saybrook, CT: Konecky and Konecky, 1942 ed.

Sargent, F. W. *England, the United States, and the Southern Confederacy*. London, UK: Sampson Low, Son, and Co., 1863.

Scharf, John Thomas. *History of the Confederate Navy, From Its Organization to the Surrender of Its Last Vessel*. Albany, NY: Joseph McDonough, 1894.

Schlüter, Herman. *Lincoln, Labor and Slavery: A Chapter from the Social History of America*. New York, NY: Socialist Literature Co., 1913.

Schurz, Carl. *Life of Henry Clay*. 2 vols. 1887. Boston, MA: Houghton, Mifflin and Co., 1899 ed.

Scott, James Brown. *James Madison's Notes of Debates in the Federal Convention of 1787, and Their Relation to a More Perfect Society of Nations*. New York, NY: Oxford University Press, 1918.

Scruggs, *The Un-Civil War: Truths Your Teacher Never Told You*. Hendersonville, NC: Tribune Papers, 2007.

Seabrook, Lochlainn. *Abraham Lincoln: The Southern View*. 2007. Franklin, TN: Sea Raven Press, 2010 ed.

——. *A Rebel Born: A Defense of Nathan Bedford Forrest, Confederate General, American Legend*. Franklin, TN: Sea Raven Press, 2010.

——. *Everything You Were Taught About the Civil War is Wrong, Ask a Southerner!* Franklin, TN: Sea Raven Press, 2010.

——. *Lincolnology: The Real Abraham Lincoln Revealed In His Own Words*. Franklin, TN: Sea Raven Press, 2011.

——. *The Unquotable Abraham Lincoln: The President's Quotes They Don't Want You To Know!* Franklin, TN: Sea Raven Press, 2011.

——. *The Quotable Jefferson Davis: Selections From the Writings and Speeches of the Confederacy's First President*. Franklin, TN: Sea Raven Press, 2012.

——. *The Quotable Robert E. Lee: Selections From the Writings and Speeches of the South's Most Beloved Civil War General*. Franklin, TN: Sea Raven Press, 2011.

——. *The Old Rebel: Robert E. Lee As He Was Seen By His Contemporaries*. Franklin, TN: Sea Raven Press, 2012.

——. *The Quotable Nathan Bedford Forrest: Selections From the Writings and Speeches of the Confederacy's Most Brilliant Cavalryman*. Franklin, TN: Sea Raven Press, 2012.

——. *Honest Jeff and Dishonest Abe: A Southern Children's Guide to the Civil War*. Franklin, TN: Sea Raven Press, 2012.

——. *The Quotable Stonewall Jackson: Selections From the Writings and Speeches of the South's Most Famous General.* Franklin, TN: Sea Raven Press, 2012.

——. *The Alexander H. Stephens Reader: Excerpts From the Works of a Confederate Founding Father.* Franklin, TN: Sea Raven Press, 2013.

——. *Everything You Were Taught About American Slavery is Wrong, Ask a Southerner!* Franklin, TN: Sea Raven Press, 2014.

——. *Confederacy 101: Amazing Facts You Never Knew About America's Oldest Political Tradition.* Franklin, TN: Sea Raven Press, 2015.

——. *The Great Yankee Coverup: What the North Doesn't Want You to Know About Lincoln's War.* Franklin, TN: Sea Raven Press, 2015.

——. *Confederate Flag Facts: What Every American Should Know About Dixie's Southern Cross.* Franklin, TN: Sea Raven Press, 2015.

Semmes, Admiral Ralph. *Service Afloat, or the Remarkable Career of the Confederate Cruisers Sumter and Alabama During the War Between the States.* London, UK: Sampson Low, Marston, Searle, and Rivington, 1887.

Sherman, William Tecumseh. *Memoirs of General William T. Sherman.* 2 vols. 1875. New York, NY: D. Appleton and Co., 1891 ed.

Simpson, Lewis P. (ed.). *I'll Take My Stand: The South and the Agrarian Tradition.* 1930. Baton Rouge, LA: University of Louisiana Press, 1977 ed.

Smelser, Marshall. *American Colonial and Revolutionary History.* 1950. New York, NY: Barnes and Noble, 1966 ed.

——. *The Democratic Republic, 1801-1815.* New York, NY: Harper and Row, 1968.

Smucker, Samuel M. *The Life and Times of Thomas Jefferson.* Philadelphia, PA: J. W. Bradley, 1859.

Sobel, Robert (ed.). *Biographical Directory of the United States Executive Branch, 1774-1898.* Westport, CT: Greenwood Press, 1990.

Spaeth, Harold J., and Edward Conrad Smith. *The Constitution of the United States.* 1936. New York, NY: HarperCollins, 1991 ed.

Spence, James. *On the Recognition of the Southern Confederation.* Ithaca, NY: Cornell University Library, 1862.

Spooner, Lysander. *No Treason* (only Numbers 1, 2, and 6 were published). Boston, MA: Lysander Spooner, 1867-1870.

Staudenraus, P. J. *The African Colonization Movement, 1816-1865.* New York, NY: Columbia University Press, 1961.

Stedman, Edmund Clarence, and Ellen Mackay Hutchinson (eds.). *A Library of American Literature From the Earliest Settlement to the Present Time.* 10 vols. New York, NY: Charles L. Webster and Co., 1888.

Steele, Joel Dorman, and Esther Baker Steele. *Barnes' Popular History of the United States of America.* New York, NY: A. S. Barnes and Co., 1904.

Stein, Ben, and Phil DeMuth. *How To Ruin the United States of America.* Carlsbad, CA: New Beginnings Press, 2008.

Stephens, Alexander Hamilton. *Speech of Mr. Stephens, of Georgia, on the War and Taxation.* Washington, D.C.: J & G. Gideon, 1848.

——. *A Constitutional View of the Late War Between the States; Its Causes, Character, Conduct and Results.* 2 vols. Philadelphia, PA: National Publishing, Co., 1870.

——. *Recollections of Alexander H. Stephens: His Diary Kept When a Prisoner at Fort Warren, Boston Harbour, 1865.* New York, NY: Doubleday, Page, and Co., 1910.

Stonebraker, J. Clarence. *The Unwritten South: Cause, Progress and Results of the Civil War - Relics of Hidden Truth After Forty Years.* Seventh ed., n.p., 1908.

Stovall, Pleasant A. *Robert Toombs: Statesman, Speaker, Soldier, Sage.* New York, NY: Cassell Publishing, 1892.

Strode, Hudson. *Jefferson Davis: American Patriot.* 3 vols. New York, NY: Harcourt, Brace and

World, 1955, 1959, 1964.

Sword, Wiley. *Southern Invincibility: A History of the Confederate Heart*. New York, NY: St. Martin's Press, 1999.

Tatalovich, Raymond, and Byron W. Daynes. *Presidential Power in the United States*. Monterey, CA: Brooks/Cole, 1984.

Taylor, Richard. *Destruction and Reconstruction: Personal Experiences of the Late War in the United States*. New York, NY: D. Appleton, 1879.

Tenney, William Jewett. *The Military and Naval History of the Rebellion in the United States*. New York, NY: D. Appleton and Co., 1865.

The American Annual Cyclopedia and Register of Important Events of the Year 1861. New York, NY: D. Appleton and Co., 1868.

The Congressional Globe, Containing Sketches of the Debates and Proceedings of the First Session of the Twenty-Eighth Congress (Vol. 13). Washington, D.C.: The Globe, 1844.

The Great Issue to be Decided in November Next: Shall the Constitution and the Union Stand or Fall, Shall Sectionalism Triumph? Washington, D.C.: National Democratic Executive Committee, 1860.

Thornton, Gordon. *The Southern Nation: The New Rise of the Old South*. Gretna, LA: Pelican Publishing Co., 2000.

Tilley, John Shipley. *Lincoln Takes Command*. 1941. Nashville, TN: Bill Coats Limited, 1991 ed.

——. *Facts the Historians Leave Out: A Confederate Primer*. 1951. Nashville, TN: Bill Coats Limited, 1999 ed.

Tocqueville, Alexis de. *Democracy in America*. 2 vols. 1836. New York, NY: D. Appleton and Co., 1904 ed.

Tourgee, Albion W. *A Fool's Errand By One of the Fools*. London, UK: George Routledge and Sons, 1883.

Tyler, Lyon Gardiner. *The Gray Book: A Confederate Catechism*. Columbia, TN: Gray Book Committee, SCV, 1935.

——. *Propaganda in History*. Richmond, VA: Richmond Press, 1920.

Upshur, Abel Parker. *A Brief Enquiry Into the True Nature and Character of Our Federal Government*. Philadelphia, PA: John Campbell, 1863.

Vallandigham, Clement Laird. *Speeches, Arguments, Addresses, and Letters of Clement L. Vallandigham*. New York, NY: J. Walter and Co., 1864.

Vanauken, Sheldon. *The Glittering Illusion: English Sympathy for the Southern Confederacy*. Washington, D.C.: Regnery, 1989.

Ver Steeg, Clarence Lester, and Richard Hofstadter. *A People and a Nation*. New York, NY: Harper and Row, 1977.

Wallcut, R. F. (pub.). *Southern Hatred of the American Government, the People of the North, and Free Institutions*. Boston, MA: R. F. Wallcut, 1862.

Warner, Ezra J. *Generals in Gray: Lives of the Confederate Commanders*. 1959. Baton Rouge, LA: Louisiana State University Press, 1989 ed.

——. *Generals in Blue: Lives of the Union Commanders*. 1964. Baton Rouge, LA: Louisiana State University Press, 2006 ed.

Washington, Henry Augustine. *The Writings of Thomas Jefferson*. 9 vols. New York, NY: H. W. Derby, 1861.

Weber, Jennifer L. *Copperheads: The Rise and Fall of Lincoln's Opponents in the North*. New York, NY: Oxford University Press, 2006.

Weintraub, Max. *The Blue Book of American History*. New York, NY: Regents Publishing Co., 1960.

Welles, Gideon. *Diary of Gideon Welles, Secretary of the Navy Under Lincoln and Johnson* (Vol. 1). Boston, MA: Houghton Mifflin, 1911.

White, Henry Alexander. *Robert E. Lee and the Southern Confederacy, 1807-1870*. New York, NY: G. P. Putnam's Sons, 1897.

Wilbur, Henry Watson. *President Lincoln's Attitude Towards Slavery and Emancipation: With a Review of Events Before and Since the Civil War*. Philadelphia, PA: W. H. Jenkins, 1914.

Wiley, Bell Irvin. *Southern Negroes: 1861-1865*. 1938. New Haven, CT: Yale University Press, 1969 ed.

——. *The Life of Johnny Reb: The Common Soldier of the Confederacy*. 1943. Baton Rouge, LA: Louisiana State University Press, 1978 ed.

——. *The Plain People of the Confederacy*. 1943. Columbia, SC: University of South Carolina, 2000 ed.

——. *The Life of Billy Yank: The Common Soldier of the Union*. 1952. Baton Rouge, LA: Louisiana State University Press, 2001 ed.

Wilkens, J. Steven. *America: The First 350 Years*. Monroe, LA: Covenant Publications, 1998.

Williams, James. *The South Vindicated*. London, UK: Longman, Green, Longman, Roberts, and Green, 1862.

Wilson, Clyde N. *Why the South Will Survive: Fifteen Southerners Look at Their Region a Half Century After I'll Take My Stand*. Athens, GA: University of Georgia Press, 1981.

——. (ed.) *The Essential Calhoun: Selections From Writings, Speeches, and Letters*. New Brunswick, NJ: Transaction Publishers, 1991.

——. *A Defender of Southern Conservatism: M.E. Bradford and His Achievements*. Columbia, MO: University of Missouri Press, 1999.

——. *From Union to Empire: Essays in the Jeffersonian Tradition*. Columbia, SC: The Foundation for American Education, 2003.

——. *Defending Dixie: Essays in Southern History and Culture*. Columbia, SC: The Foundation for American Education, 2005.

Wilson, Woodrow. *Division and Reunion: 1829-1889*. 1893. New York, NY: Longmans, Green, and Co., 1908 ed.

——. *A History of the American People*. 5 vols. 1902. New York, NY: Harper and Brothers, 1918 ed.

Woods, Thomas E., Jr. *The Politically Incorrect Guide to American History*. Washington, D.C.: Regnery, 2004.

Woodworth, Steven E. *Jefferson Davis and His Generals: The Failure of Confederate Command in the West*. Lawrence, KS: University Press of Kansas, 1990.

Zavodnyik, Peter. *The Age of Strict Construction: A History of the Growth of Federal Power, 1789-1861*. Washington, D.C.: Catholic University of America Press, 2007.

Zinn, Howard. *A People's History of the United States: 1492-Present*. 1980. New York, NY: HarperCollins, 1995.

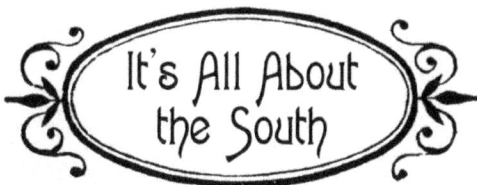

It's All About the South

Lincoln's War was nothing more than a military continuation of the age-old fight between conservatism and liberalism; in this case, between Northern Liberals and Southern Conservatives. Progressive Yankees, like Lincoln, did not like the limitations placed on the government by the Founding Fathers in the US Constitution and sought to overturn them. Traditional Southerners, like Davis, on the other hand, believed (correctly) that the US Constitution and its many laws are what make our country unique and the greatest among the world's many nations. In essence then, the South seceded in order to preserve the original US Constitution as set forth by the Founders, which resulted in the creation of the Constitution of the CSA in 1861; the North fought in order to overturn the US Constitution and give more power to the central government. America's "Civil War" continues to this day.

Index

OCHLAINN SEABROOK, winner of the prestigious Jefferson Davis Historical Gold Medal for his "masterpiece," *A Rebel Born: A Defense of Nathan Bedford Forrest*, is an unreconstructed Southern historian, award-winning author, Civil War scholar, and traditional Southern Agrarian of Scottish, English, Irish, Dutch, Welsh, German, and Italian extraction. An encyclopedist, lexicographer, musician, artist, graphic designer, genealogist, and photographer, as well as an award-winning poet, songwriter, and screenwriter, he has a 40 year background in historical nonfiction writing and is a member of the Sons of Confederate Veterans, the Civil War Trust, and the National Grange.

Due to similarities in their writing styles, ideas, and literary works, Seabrook is often referred to as the "new Shelby Foote," the "Southern Joseph Campbell," and the "American Robert Graves" (his English cousin).

The grandson of an Appalachian coal-mining family, Seabrook is a seventh-generation Kentuckian, co-chair of the Jent/Gent Family Committee (Kentucky), founder and director of the Blakeney Family Tree Project, and a board member of the Friends of Colonel Benjamin E. Caudill. Seabrook's literary works have been endorsed by leading authorities, museum curators, award-winning historians, bestselling authors, celebrities, noted scientists, well respected educators, TV show hosts

COPYRIGHT ©
SEA RAVEN PRESS

Lochlainn Seabrook, award-winning Civil War scholar and unreconstructed Southern historian, is America's most popular and prolific pro-South author.

and producers, renowned military artists, esteemed Southern organizations, and distinguished academicians from around the world.

Seabrook has authored over 45 popular adult books on the American Civil War, American and international slavery, the U.S. Confederacy (1781), the Southern Confederacy (1861), religion, theology and thealogy, Jesus, the Bible, the Apocrypha, the Law of Attraction, alternative health, spirituality, ghost stories, the paranormal, ufology, social issues, and cross-cultural studies of the family and marriage. His Confederate biographies, pro-South studies, genealogical monographs, family histories, military encyclopedias, self-help guides, and etymological dictionaries have received wide acclaim.

Seabrook's eight children's books include a Southern guide to the Civil War, a biography of Nathan Bedford Forrest, a dictionary of religion and myth, a rewriting of the King Arthur legend (which reinstates the original pre-Christian motifs), two bedtime stories for preschoolers, a naturalist's guidebook to owls, a worldwide look at the family, and an examination of the Near-Death Experience.

Of blue-blooded Southern stock through his Kentucky, Tennessee, Virginia, West Virginia, and North Carolina ancestors, he is a direct descendant of European royalty via his 6th great-grandfather, the Earl of Oxford, after which London's famous Harley Street is named. Among his celebrated male Celtic ancestors is Robert the Bruce, King of Scotland, Seabrook's 22nd great-grandfather. The 21st great-grandson of Edward I "Longshanks" Plantagenet), King of England, Seabrook is a thirteenth-generation Southerner through his descent from the colonists of Jamestown, Virginia (1607).

The 2nd, 3rd, and 4th great-grandson of dozens of Confederate soldiers, one of his closest connections to Lincoln's War is through his 3rd great-grandfather, Elias Jent, Sr., who fought for the Confederacy in the Thirteenth Cavalry Kentucky under Seabrook's 2nd cousin, Colonel Benjamin E. Caudill. The Thirteenth, also known as "Caudill's Army," fought in numerous conflicts, including the Battles of Saltville, Gladsville, Mill Cliff, Poor Fork, Whitesburg, and Leatherwood.

Seabrook is a direct descendant of the families of Alexander H. Stephens, John Singleton Mosby, William Giles Harding, and Edmund Winchester Rucker, and is related to the following Confederates and other 18th- and 19th-Century luminaries: Robert E. Lee, Stephen Dill

Lee, Stonewall Jackson, Nathan Bedford Forrest, James Longstreet, John Hunt Morgan, Jeb Stuart, Pierre G. T. Beauregard (approved the Confederate Battle Flag design), George Washington Gordon, John Bell Hood, Alexander Peter Stewart, Arthur M. Manigault, Joseph Manigault, Charles Scott Venable, Thornton A. Washington, John A. Washington, Abraham Buford, Edmund W. Pettus, Theodrick "Tod" Carter, John B. Womack, John H. Winder, Gideon J. Pillow, States Rights Gist, Henry R. Jackson, John Lawton Seabrook, John C. Breckinridge, Leonidas Polk, Zachary Taylor, Sarah Knox Taylor (first wife of Jefferson Davis), Richard Taylor, Davy Crockett, Daniel Boone, Meriwether Lewis (of the Lewis and Clark Expedition) Andrew Jackson, James K. Polk, Abram Poindexter Maury (founder of Franklin, TN), Zebulon Vance, Thomas Jefferson, Edmund Jennings Randolph, George Wythe Randolph (grandson of Jefferson), Felix K. Zollicoffer, Fitzhugh Lee, Nathaniel F. Cheairs, Jesse James, Frank James, Robert Brank Vance, Charles Sidney Winder, John W. McGavock, Caroline E. (Winder) McGavock, David Harding McGavock, Lysander McGavock, James Randal McGavock, Randal William McGavock, Francis McGavock, Emily McGavock, William Henry F. Lee, Lucius E. Polk, Minor Meriwether (husband of noted pro-South author Elizabeth Avery Meriwether), Ellen Bourne Tynes (wife of Forrest's chief of artillery, Captain John W. Morton), South Carolina Senators Preston Smith Brooks and Andrew Pickens Butler, and famed South Carolina diarist Mary Chesnut.

Seabrook's modern day cousins include: Patrick J. Buchanan (conservative author), Cindy Crawford (model), Shelby Lee Adams (Letcher Co., Kentucky, photographer), Bertram Thomas Combs (Kentucky's 50th governor), Edith Bolling (wife of President Woodrow Wilson), and actors Andy Griffith, George C. Scott, Robert Duvall, Reese Witherspoon, Lee Marvin, Rebecca Gayheart, and Tom Cruise.

Seabrook's screenplay, *A Rebel Born*, based on his book of the same name, has been signed with acclaimed filmmaker Christopher Forbes (of Forbes Film). It is now in pre-production, and is set for release in 2017 as a full-length feature film. This will be the first movie ever made of Nathan Bedford Forrest's life story, and as a historically accurate project written from the Southern perspective, is destined to be one of the most talked about Civil War films of all time.

Born with music in his blood, Seabrook is an award-winning, multi-genre, BMI-Nashville songwriter and lyricist who has composed some 3,000 songs (250 albums), and whose original music has been heard in film (*A Rebel Born, Cowgirls 'n Angels, Confederate Cavalry, Billy the Kid: Showdown in Lincoln County, Vengeance Without Mercy, Last Step, County Line, The Mark*) and on TV and radio worldwide. A musician, producer, multi-instrumentalist, and renown performer—whose keyboard work has been variously compared to pianists from Hargus Robbins and Vince Guaraldi to Elton John and Leonard Bernstein—Seabrook has opened for groups such as the Earl Scruggs Review, Ted Nugent, and Bob Seger, and has performed privately for such public figures as President Ronald Reagan, Burt Reynolds, Loni Anderson, and Senator Edward W. Brooke. Seabrook's cousins in the music business include: Johnny Cash, Elvis Presley, Billy Ray and Miley Cyrus, Patty Loveless, Tim McGraw, Lee Ann Womack, Dolly Parton, Pat Boone, Naomi, Wynonna, and Ashley Judd, Ricky Skaggs, the Sunshine Sisters, Martha Carson, and Chet Atkins.

(Photo © Lochlainn Seabrook)

Seabrook, a libertarian, lives with his wife and family in historic Middle Tennessee, the heart of Forrest country and the Confederacy, where his conservative Southern ancestors fought valiantly against Liberal Lincoln and the progressive North in defense of Jeffersonianism, constitutional government, and personal liberty.

LochlainnSeabrook.com

If you enjoyed this book you will be interested in Mr. Seabrook's other popular related titles:

☛ EVERYTHING YOU WERE TAUGHT ABOUT THE CIVIL WAR IS WRONG, ASK A SOUTHERNER!
☛ EVERYTHING YOU WERE TAUGHT ABOUT AMERICAN SLAVERY IS WRONG, ASK A SOUTHERNER!
☛ THE GREAT YANKEE COVERUP: WHAT THE NORTH DOESN'T WANT YOU TO KNOW ABOUT LINCOLN'S WAR!
☛ CONFEDERATE FLAG FACTS: WHAT EVERY AMERICAN SHOULD KNOW ABOUT DIXIE'S SOUTHERN CROSS

Available from Sea Raven Press and wherever fine books are sold

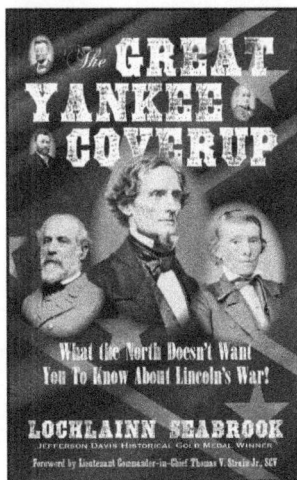

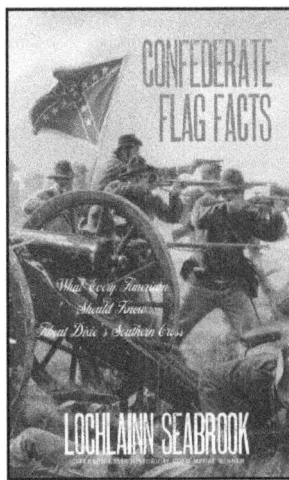

ALL OF OUR BOOK COVERS ARE AVAILABLE AS 11" X 17" POSTERS, SUITABLE FOR FRAMING.

SeaRavenPress.com